How does a company get the kind of information it needs to make strategic decisions? Informal, around-the-water-cooler methods aren't good enough when the stakes are high and the outcomes can mean the difference between an organization's success or failure. What's needed, say intelligence experts Tamar Gilad and Benjamin Gilad, is a formal, on-going *system* to collect, analyze, and report business intelligence.

With a structured BI program, you are better able to:

- Track current and potential competitors
- Analyze markets
- Develop profitable new products
- Determine likely candidates for acquisition or merger
- Monitor technological developments

and keep abreast of a broad range of political, economic, social, and legislative trends with significant impact on your company's fortunes.

The Business Intelligence System: A New Tool for Competitive Advantage offers the first complete, professional approach to intelligence management. It shows you how to:

- Set targets for a BI program and determine *your* organization's critical intelligence needs
- Establish an intelligence collection network, using your own employees and internal resources — an approach that's both productive and economical
- Tap the best external information sources: publications, government documents, court records, computerized data bases, conferences and trade shows, customers, suppliers, and many more
- Evaluate the quality and reliability of collected data, to reduce the flood of information to useful "building blocks" that meet the needs of different groups in your company

- Design and manage systems for information storage and dissemination, taking advantage of computer capabilities
- Determine the best organizational structure for your BI system
- Recognize and overcome common problems in intelligence gathering

Complete with useful forms and checklists, **The Business Intelligence System** provides a major resource for planning executives, directors of new business development, marketing and market research staff, and all managers involved in guiding their organizations to greater profitability.

THE
BUSINESS
INTELLIGENCE
SYSTEM

THE BUSINESS INTELLIGENCE SYSTEM

A New Tool for Competitive Advantage

Benjamin Gilad
Tamar Gilad

90-2541

amacom

American Management Association

Library of Congress Cataloging-in-Publication Data

Gilad, Benjamin.
    The business intelligence system.

    Bibliography: p.
    Includes index.
    1. Business intelligence. I. Gilad, Tamar. II. Title.
HD38.7.G55   1988   658.4'7   87-47827
ISBN 0-8144-5929-3

Printing number

10 9 8 7 6 5 4 3 2 1

To
Cindy,
my true inspiration,
without whom this book would not have been written—
with love

To
Maya Leah,
despite whose best efforts this book was
nonetheless written

Preface

Things are not what they used to be for the American corporation. The current business climate represents a drastic change from even a decade ago. The most important change, undoubtedly, is the rise in the degree of competition, both foreign and domestic.

During the 60s and early 70s, when the business environment was relatively stable, the new management tool of strategic planning gained wide acceptance in the corridors of corporations and business schools. It was easy to plan when you could successfully predict economic trends and accurately guess how competitors and consumers would react.

But the business picture gradually changed. During the 70s, competitive pressures mounted rapidly, and American corporations began to lose their hegemony in world and even domestic markets. Management experts responded with a new tool, that of competitive analysis, which is now almost as popular as strategic planning was earlier. Favored by large companies in the U.S., as well as companies abroad, competitive analysis was based on the novel idea that good management must track developments in the business environment and what the competition was doing. This was quite a change from the naive managerial attitude that "a darn good product is all one needs in this business."

Now, as we approach the 1990s, the economic pressures are stronger than ever. Some economists are talking about the deindustrialization of America, while others see little chance for the American corporation to grow in the face of international competition. We don't subscribe to the doomsday prophecies. Yet, we do believe that the business environment is changing so rapidly that the old managerial tools no longer suffice. In the 60s the name of the game was "The sky's the limit"; in the 70s it was "Just hold the line"; today it's "Let's just survive."

How do you play to survive? Certainly not by being overconfident. Surviving in these turbulent times requires the adoption of new management techniques and aggressive strategies. One excellent tool is business intelligence. History teaches that behind every successful strategy there has been a tireless effort to collect intelligence. IBM proved it. GE has been doing it. And the Japanese are the masters of the art. It's time for every manager to become acquainted with the use of business intelligence.

Business intelligence is *not* industrial espionage. The latter is an overrated and largely ineffective—not to mention illegal—way of gaining temporary access to the golden egg, used by those who lack the skill to raise the right goose. Business intelligence (BI) is a legitimate organizational activity, which occurs to one degree or another in every firm. The definition of BI we employ is as follows:

> BI is the activity of monitoring the environment external to the firm for information that is relevant for the decision-making process in the company.

There are two ways to carry out BI activities: formally and informally. Informal BI involves uncoordinated BI activities carried on by individuals on an ad hoc basis. A formal BI process is organized, systematic, and ongoing, and it produces high quality intelligence. It is not very effective to devote resources to formal planning while neglecting the input to the plans, that input being the business intelligence itself. Moreover, in a turbulent environment, there is no other way to prepare against threats, or to identify opportunities early on, than to systematically, seriously, and competently monitor the environment. That cannot be done well without a BI system.

This book shows how to build an effective BI system in an organization. The system outlined here is based on principles of military intelligence, which are similar to the principles of business intelligence, although the ethics are very different. To date, we have taught the principles of BI to hundreds of executives across the U.S., and have found their interest and enthusiasm surprisingly high. For that reason, we have decided to write a step-by-step BI handbook so that you can benefit from the lessons we have gained from countless discussions, work groups, and consultations with various organizations here and abroad.

You will note as you read that the identity of companies portrayed in the examples throughout the text has been disguised. Nevertheless, you should be aware that the cases are based on our interaction with hundreds of executives across the U.S. and abroad who are currently involved with establishing and managing BI programs.

This book is written for two distinct groups. The first group consists of those involved in setting the direction for a firm, and those executives who play a significant role in the planning process, such as CEOs, presidents, planning VPs, marketing directors, and business development executives. For these executives, we believe a knowledge of the principles of formal BI is invaluable, and should help them decide if and how to institute such a system in their organizations. The other group comprises executives and professionals whose main responsibility includes the handling of information, from competitive to technological, and who are, in fact, in charge of gathering business intelligence for their companies.

Whichever group you belong to, we hope you will find the advice in this book to be valuable for your firm.

Tamar Gilad and Benjamin Gilad

Contents

1

The Nature and Domain of Business Intelligence Activities

The term BI is used to denote a process, an organizational function, and a product. The process or activity of BI, which is carried out by individuals or by a formal organizational unit, produces a product that is termed business intelligence. The best definition we found for this end product is Greene's (1966), who defines the BI product as the "processed information of interest to management about the present and future environment in which the business is operating."

While the definition is broad, it captures the essence of BI. First, the emphasis in the BI product is on *processed* information. We distinguish here between data—the raw material that is composed of facts—and intelligence, which is information digested, analyzed, and interpreted for the purpose of decision making.

Second, the definition points to *management* as having a crucial role in BI. Management decides what will be in the domain of BI, by determining what information is of interest or relevance to its decisions. Moreover, management's involvement determines whether the BI process will yield intelligence, or whether the process will yield a

1

second Library of Congress collection. (The issue of management involvement will be discussed in detail throughout the book.)

Finally, BI is concerned with the company's *environment*, both the present environment (mostly for tactical intelligence) and the future environment (mostly for strategic intelligence). In their day-to-day operations, corporations rely constantly on BI for tactical decisions in promotion mix, for instance. The purpose of a formal BI system is to shift the emphasis from reliance on short-term tactical intelligence to better use of strategic intelligence in the decision-making process. A strategic orientation to the business intelligence program requires that historical data are used circumspectly, and only if they can shed light on future developments. Historical data or simple trend extrapolation from historical data are primarily an indication of past performance and are unlikely to produce assessments that are insightful or indicative of future opportunities.

Many more companies are now realizing that a true strategic orientation requires that they abandon the simplistic quantitative models of past history in favor of a more realistic, complex view of their competitive environment and its future trends. For example, a large office products company completely turned around the way it had been conducting the strategic planning process when it perceived the inadequacy of its method of historical extrapolations. The company's initial goal for its ten-year strategic planning effort was to project several potential worldwide revenue quotas for the company in its key markets. The project was carried out by corporate staff who took advantage of the sophisticated techniques and projection methods used by research institutions such as the Rand Corporation. The results of this planning process were reported in a 300-page document. The report, predictably, had little discernible impact on the strategy of the corporation. The company's most recent ten-year planning effort focused on analyzing the external environment. It took advantage of the knowledge of line management in its operating units by including a bottom-up view of the company's markets, as well as a top-down corporate perspective. Through progressively more focused analysis meetings, top management, with input from its operating units, developed a consensus of the future environment. Rather than generating a useless mathematical exercise, the company had arrived at a practical, useful scenario for the future.

Strategic intelligence calls for greater scope, depth, and sophistication of input and analysis than tactical intelligence. Strategic intelligence requires therefore the institutionalization of the BI process, by which we mean the building of a BI system as a legitimate organizational resource.

Here's another example: A few years ago, Mobil Corporation embarked on an acquisition campaign that resulted, among other acquisitions, in the purchase of Montgomery Ward, the retail merchandise chain. This acquisition was the result of a strategic attempt to diversify away from energy-related products at a time when Mobil's dependence on Arab oil had become a risk more than an asset. It appears that in this case, Mobil's intelligence effort in finding out the competitive position of Montgomery Ward left much to be desired. Montgomery Ward, as it turned out, was years behind in its policies and its image. This information, which was known to analysts in the industry and which could have been verified with some BI investigation of competitors such as Sears and K-MART, was either not collected by Mobil or simply ignored. Thus Mobil paid a high price for a company with deep-rooted problems. Such strategic decisions as acquisitions, competitive positioning, and product development, to mention only a few, cannot and should not be made with shoddy "legwork." The stakes demand a professional approach to intelligence collection.

A common myth about the BI product, which should be dispelled early on, is that there is a linear relationship between its availability and a company's expenditure on BI activities. But, as every experienced intelligence expert knows, some BI products cost nothing to obtain—the intelligence is obtained as an unintended by-product of other activities. For example, intelligence obtained by executives during a golf game is a by-product of the activity. Similarly, competitor intelligence obtained by a salesperson in the field is a by-product of the selling activity. Other excellent intelligence pieces may cost very little, such as a "subscription" to a competitor's internal newsletter. On the other hand, some intelligence, such as a competitor's strategic plans, cannot be legally obtained at any price, and management should not expect to obtain such intelligence. An effective intelligence system provides management with enough input to make intelligent decisions at a cost not exceeding the value of the intelligence.

An example of a moderate-cost BI system in a high-stakes game, which yielded large incremental benefits, is that of a company that wanted to estimate as accurately as possible at what price a competitor would bid for a government defense project. Of course, obtaining the information directly was impossible. But the company instituted a BI program that resulted, over time, and through the collection of many bits and pieces of data, in the piecing together of a picture of the rival's cost structure, its management priorities and commitments, and other indicators that helped it to arrive at an estimate of the competitor's bids. Eventually, it was able to outbid the competitor on an important project.

Another misconception regarding BI is the confusion of BI activities with industrial espionage, a confusion that alienates many honest executives and even prevents them from thinking logically about BI. To clarify the distinction between the two it is necessary to define both activities explicitly. BI concerns the *ethical* gathering and use of publicly or semipublicly available information as a basis for planning. Publicly available information refers mainly to published data to which the public has access. Semipublic information refers to data obtained from the field, such as information from customers, suppliers, peers, and others.

Industrial espionage is the use of illegal and immoral techniques to collect information—such as trade secrets—not voluntarily provided by the source. This is the distinction between Hitachi's stealing of IBM's designs by bribing employees and the legitimate gathering of intelligence by Japanese trade representatives on tours of U.S. plants, tours that were organized by the U.S. firms themselves. In business intelligence, information is collected by asking the right questions of the right sources, but never by coercing individuals to give answers. What is not provided freely by a source cannot be collected legally or morally. There is nothing immoral or illegal, however, in asking questions. The litmus test for the collector of intelligence is that there be no fear of public condemnation were the actions published on the front page of a newspaper. If you were willing to read about your methods in the press, they would presumably be defensible on moral and legal grounds.

Despite this clear distinction between BI and industrial espionage, real-life situations are often ambiguous. We were once asked by an executive of a consumer electronics company to define the following case in which he was involved. A young engineer working for one of his competitors showed up in his office one day for a job interview. In the course of the interview the engineer pulled out a set of blueprints of the competitor's new product, on which he had been working, and offered them to our client. Should he have accepted the blueprints? Was it a case of BI or industrial espionage?

An analysis of this case does not yield an unequivocal answer.

On the one hand it is BI—the engineer provided the information by his own volition. On the other hand, he had defrauded his employer by revealing the plans, and therefore accepting them would have made our client a partner in crime. We asked the executive how he had reacted to the situation and he answered that he had refused the offer and did not hire the applicant. His reason was that if the engineer had transgressed once, he would do it again. Besides, he didn't like disloyal people.

This answer suggests the best test in gauging the morality of an intelligence collecting activity. Since we believe that personal and business morality should be identical (that is, that one should apply the same principles of moral judgment to personal and professional situations), the ultimate test for the appropriateness of an act must be subjective. Does it feel right? If it does, but only in a "this is business" context, we believe the activity should be shunned, even if good intelligence is lost. After all, your integrity should be worth more than a piece of information. (See the chapter on legal, moral, and counterintelligence issues for examples of other cases.)

Now that the basic terms have been defined, we can proceed to the more technical material pertaining to BI as a process, and the systems that can be used to carry on the BI activity.

The Scope of BI Activity

The system used to perform the BI activity seeks to provide information about the company's external environment. This information is an integral part of the organization's total information system. It augments the internal information generated by the routine operation of the business. The scope of intelligence operations depends upon both the needs of the corporation and the allocation of resources to the BI activity, very much like the way a corporation defines the scope of its accounting system in accordance with its control requirements. The Tandem Corporation, a company operating in a competitive setting, Gulf Oil, a multinational corporation, and General Motors, a corporation that depends heavily on predicting certain developments (for example, governmental regulation), will have BI systems different in scope and nature than Container Corporation of America, a company in a stable, mature industry.

The broadest scope of a BI system is offered by the concept of

environmental scanning, which was popularized in the 70s by Aguilar (1967). In practice, however, most corporations that employ a
rudimentary BI operation concentrate on current competitors. The
following list presents a sample of possible areas of BI coverage.
Naturally, the ideal coverage can be determined only on a case-by-
case basis.

The Domain of Business Intelligence

Current competitors	Economic environment
Potential competition	Social and community
Growth opportunities	environment
Technological environment	Demographics
Markets	Suppliers
Political and regulatory	Acquisition candidates
environment	

Each of these areas entails the collection of different kinds of information. For example, to track competitors, information will be collected about their strategies, plans, resources, goals, strengths, weaknesses, and actions. To analyze markets, information will be gathered
about such factors as market potential, customer needs, tastes, and
preferences, and promotion response. A coverage of the technological environment will entail gathering information about present and
potential product and process technologies. Understandably, the
regulatory environment will be monitored by tracking government
legislation, the state, and federal regulatory agencies.

The scope of BI monitoring depends upon the needs of the
corporation and the allocation of resources to the business intelligence function. Thus, if a division with limited resources is setting
up a system, it may not be able to assign more than one part-time
person to the task. Therefore the scope of coverage may be limited to
current competitors and perhaps to monitoring technological developments, especially if the business relies for its success on the ability
to stay abreast of rapidly changing technology. A multinational
corporation with business in many different countries will probably
need to monitor the political environment in each of the major
countries where it does business. Again, if a company does business
in a mature, stagnant market, it may not need to cover potential
competition because it is highly unlikely that new entrants will be

interested in their market. There may even be less of a pressing need to monitor existing competitors closely. Its main objective, however, may be to diversify away from the existing market, which may mean scanning the environment for profitable industries and acquisition candidates.

Determining accurately the scope of the business intelligence system is important because the system has to provide information to support decision making in the organization. A system that follows conventions and attempts to emulate what everyone else does may be a system that misses its mission. Deciding on the scope should be the first consideration in setting up a BI operation. From that will follow the choosing of specific intelligence collection targets and the planning of the collection and analysis functions.

Consumer goods companies are known to have sophisticated market research departments. Market research has also become commonplace among producers of industrial goods. Many companies also monitor their immediate competitors and all companies who have set up formal business intelligence systems gear the system to monitor their major competitors. However, some industries are dynamic and fast changing, and their environment poses many discontinuities. These discontinuities are often produced by technological breakthroughs, by regulatory actions, and by environmental events that are highly unpredictable, such as acquisitions. For such industries it is very important to scan the environment beyond the traditional domain of market research and beyond closely watching the moves of competitors. For example, the marketing department of a technology-based company conducted a market research survey of its product and compared the product, its features and price, to competing products in the same segment. The results were encouraging: The company's product had more features and a lower price. The marketing department concluded that the company enjoyed a firm and favorable competitive position. Had their search for information carried them beyond traditional market research they would have found indications that one of their major competitors was developing a third-generation product that was far more advanced than what they themselves had on the drawing board. This information would have made them much less complacent than they were after the market survey. In fact, a year later the competitor introduced its new product, which very rapidly caused the company to lose sales and market share.

Managers setting up a BI system should also keep in mind that

if environmental scanning is entirely limited to the current domain of
the firm, that is, to existing markets and competitors, the intelligence
on which future strategy is built will be limited to the current
activities of the firm. This will lead to strategies that are shortsighted
at their worst and incremental in nature at best. An ideal system
should therefore not be excessively limited in scope and should allow
for some broader scanning of the business environment.

Is BI the Same as Market Research?

In some corporations there is a belief that it is enough to have a good
market research department to have good BI. Although the information produced by a market research department is BI, it is only a
small part of the total BI required for decision making. The emphasis
in market research is on point-of-sale data with special attention on
the customer. Good BI includes, naturally, good knowledge of the
customer, but much more than that. The differences between market
research and BI are summarized in Table 1–1. We would like to note,
however, that in our experience market research personnel are, by
training, familiar with the methods of BI research and can therefore
serve as a core for the building of BI capability.

A Theoretical Overview:
The Different Approaches to BI Activity[1]

There are various ways to structure BI activity, depending upon the
priorities and resources of the organization. One classification of BI
activity is based on the approach it takes to the use of data. This
classification comprises three possible approaches: Dynamic data/
Static questions, Static data/Dynamic questions, and Dynamic data/
Dynamic questions.

The Dynamic data/Static questions (D/S) approach seeks to monitor an incoming flow of data by searching for answers to certain

[1]Note: The general reader may skip this section without loss of understanding. The professional practitioner, however, may wish to get a broader,
theoretical underpinning of the intelligence operation.

Table 1–1. Market research and business intelligence: A comparison.

	Market Research	Business Intelligence
Scope	Mainly customer-oriented, or sales-related information	Total external environment, especially competitive-oriented
Character	Narrow and in-depth reports regarding specific aspects of company's business as it affects sales and sales policy	Broad, continual scanning of environment for present and future opportunities and threats in all areas of company's operations
Use	For planning production levels, marketing and distribution policies	Strategic positioning, countermoves against competition, mergers, and acquisitions, R&D efforts
Time horizon	Mainly short to medium range	Short run (operational intelligence) and long run (strategic intelligence)
Sources of information	Publications, surveys, experiments, interviews	Publications, field network, internal network
Objectives	Reduce risk of product decisions	Prepare management for future environment

predetermined questions. An example of D/S is the monitoring of data for information about a competitor's capacity utilization. Data on plant openings or closings, for instance, or changes in shifts will then be identified in the stream of data collected from publications and field reports that arrive at the desk of the BI analyst.

The Static data/Dynamic questions (S/D) approach makes use of a library of existing information to answer changing questions. Any time an analyst searches an existing data base, the analyst is using an S/D approach. It does not mean that the library itself remains static. Rather, the monitoring of the incoming data is not immediate and continual (except for indexing and cataloging).

The Dynamic data/Dynamic questions (D/D) approach involves the continuous monitoring of data impinging on the firm and the active pursuit of data for answering changing questions and responding to intelligence requests that pose questions not included in the predetermined list of BI targets.

In addition to the three (not mutually exclusive) approaches to structuring BI activity, there is another classification of BI activities based on the primary purpose for which the BI activity is organized. This classification deals with defensive and offensive intelligence. Defensive intelligence is oriented toward avoiding surprises. Defensive BI is especially compatible with a Dynamic data/Static questions approach. In defensive BI the purpose of the function is to monitor incoming data to detect changes in the existing competitive situation. If a threat is detected (a change, for example, in the competitor's product mix, pricing strategy, or other predetermined variable of interest to the company), management is alerted. In the business policy field, defensive intelligence is associated with defensive management in general. A typical example is a market leader that, rather than innovate, engages in the strategy of meeting the competition to preserve its market share. Such an approach to management will emphasize defensive intelligence activities.

The primary purpose of offensive intelligence is to identify opportunities as they arise. Offensive BI is compatible with the approaches of Dynamic data/Dynamic questions and Static data/ Dynamic questions because it requires changing directions of data collection in a way that is consistent with the changing environment and with changing management goals and concerns. The broad scanning of the environment required by offensive intelligence necessitates sophisticated methods of collection. An example of the use of offensive intelligence is a case where the BI unit (BIU) alerted management to the fact that a major competitor was laying off R&D personnel of a particular specialization during a recent recession. The company then concentrated its research effort in that particular area. The situation was judged an opportunity by top management; but if the BIU had not tabbed the data as strategic intelligence of interest to management, and had not relayed the information, the opportunity might have been missed.

Formal or Informal BI?

Informal BI activity is the most common form of BI in many corporations. In every firm, large and small, executives and employees engage in some form of intelligence gathering. In fact, a famous study of CEOs once found that they devoted close to 40 percent of their time to gathering data about the competitive environment. Informal BI, then, is conducted by whoever is inclined or interested in the subject *at the time*, and may even include special, possibly large-scale projects of intelligence gathering that has been assigned to junior staff. Examples of informal BI activity abound: They include the information exchanged during executive meetings, industry gossip reported by subordinates to their bosses, even special studies made of competitor actions prior to major presentations by the planning or marketing departments.

Informal activity is inexpensive in terms of operating and set-up costs. It does not require special personnel training, outside consulting, or organizational change. In many organizations, informal collection of BI is initiated by intelligence-minded executives as an automatic step before major decisions are made, as a side activity of their interaction with other executives and subordinates, or as a spontaneous reaction to their daily reading of published material.

The major problem with informal BI is that it is not a coordinated, systematic organizational function. It falls between the cracks and is subject to the vagaries of a particular executive's needs and available time. Rather than being a powerful competitive resource, to be deployed by the management of the organization to further its goals, it depends instead on the good will of a few individuals. The lack of systematic operation causes gaps in the collection, evaluation, and analysis of BI information. Information that may be crucial to decisions may easily be overlooked when subjected to unsystematic, discontinuous monitoring. Another drawback is that in an informal, uncoordinated system, duplication of efforts and wasting of resources may result, since several people in the organization may be collecting, but not sharing, the same data. A related problem is the lack of effective dissemination. We have encountered again and again cases where one executive in the organization possessed information that was needed by another, but for lack of a formal system of dissemination the information never reached the other executive.

The second major problem with informal BI activity is the lack of corporate perspective in a diffused, locally initiated BI effort. The fact that in informal collection no one explicitly determines corporate priorities and informational needs causes such collection to be at best haphazard, and creates a bias for the collection of tactical rather than strategic intelligence. Thus, managers will keep track of their competitors' prices, advertising, and product changes. However, it is highly unlikely that they will develop comprehensive knowledge of a competitor's strategy, or monitor the technological-social-regulatory environment to the degree required for long-range planning.

The third major problem with informal BI is the risk of unethical behavior. With the lack of explicit, central guidelines on what is permissible, local initiatives can lead to illegal and immoral acts of industrial espionage. Thus, contrary to common belief, it is the institutionalization of BI that results in greater control of the ethics of the activity.

Formal BI activity—a BI system—permits the regular and continual collection, analysis, and reporting of intelligence by trained personnel, often controlled by a separate organizational BI function. The disadvantage of a formal BI system is that it is more costly than an informal one, because it involves set-up and operating costs. One purpose of this book is to teach executives how to minimize the cost of a system with the use of already available *internal* resources.

The advantages of a BI system are many. The formalizing of BI activity increases the supply of BI manyfold, both in quality and in quantity. The quantity increases simply because of the rise in *awareness* of the subject by employees. Quality improves because collection is *targeted*. Curiously enough, demand for information increases as well. Several BI managers told us that the rise in demand starts with a few simple questions that are asked by line managers almost reluctantly. Then, as the BI staff provides answers, the recipients begin asking for more. Very soon, the BI unit is swamped by requests for intelligence on "everything" and "as soon as possible." A formal BI system brings corporate perspective to both the collection and the analysis of the data. It also specifies the limits to the activity. But beyond these apparent advantages, it is simply a necessity of the times. Informal BI activity is often ineffective. At a time of challenge to traditional management practices, changes in the way some American companies handle their BI needs is essential. In Japan, BI activity is part of the organizational culture, as is clear to anyone who has accompanied or even watched a group of Japanese businessmen touring an American plant, participating in an international trade show, or attending a lecture in an American university. The "obsession" with taking pictures, which is such a familiar Japanese behavior, is a natural element in their intelligence-gathering activity. Their daily meetings of management with management, and management with employees, inside and outside the workplace, typically includes the passing of intelligence. In the U.S., where cultural and social habits are different, American executives use formalization and institutionalization as a substitute for internalization. While the Japanese worker may be an "automatic" intelligence collector for his company simply because he sees his firm as an extension of his own life, the American worker must be trained to be a BI expert with the right incentives and the effective structuring of BI activity.

The continual collection of BI is, of course, the major difference between the formal and informal activities. What makes the constant gathering process so essential is that it is rarely possible to collect all the data required for a full competitive analysis in one massive effort. Moreover, the use of a BI system for *advance* warning on critical threats and opportunities, as opposed to the collection of historical data, necessitates constant monitoring, because of the unpredictable nature of critical events.

A perfect example of colossal BI failure that occurred because of the lack of systematic monitoring of the competitive environment was the inability of the American automobile companies to recognize the changes that were taking place in the market during the 1970s; there were changes in consumer preferences regarding the size of cars, new social concerns about safety and environmental pollution, the willingness of government to legislate severe standards, and a dramatic rise in the technological and managerial abilities of the Japanese manufacturers. It is impossible to predict whether or not a BI system would have made a difference in decisions reached at the big three auto companies at the time, but it is possible to point to the rather dramatic difference in their attitude toward BI since then. The difference is expressed both in BI objectives behind joint ventures, as disclosed by a senior GM executive, and in formal BI programs.

Lastly, continual monitoring of the environment, as opposed to individual ad hoc projects, shortens the response time between the need for the information and its actual collection. When decisions that depend on intelligence are made against deadlines, a shorter response time is crucial. A good example is computer companies' annual rush to introduce new products around Christmastime. The need to predict the product-promotion mix of competitors becomes more pressing as the peak sales season nears. A formal and continuous BI monitoring program that gathers bits and pieces of information year-round can help put together the puzzle on time, since hints and clues about the competitors' intentions may become available quite early in the year. Thus, as the deadline for new product introductions nears, a formal BI program pays off.

The formalizing of BI activity is not an all-or-nothing proposition. Depending on the organization and its resources, portions of the intelligence-gathering process can be formalized while others remain informal. A complete BI system may be appropriate for an organization facing tough domestic and international competition, while only some formal collection may be needed by a small, owner-run company. The point to remember is that usually what is informal needs reinforcement through a strong corporate culture. Table 1–2, below, summarizes the major differences between formal and informal BI. Some of these differences will become clearer over the next few chapters as the actual BI process is discussed.

Final Word

A common misperception is that a formal BI system is needed, and can only be undertaken, by large corporations. This is simply not true. Small and medium-sized businesses, including divisions of larger corporations, need to know about the competition and other environmental factors just as much as, if not more than, large companies, or corporate headquarters. The resources they may be able to invest in a BI system might be limited, but that does not mean that a BI system should not be instituted. An effective system can be based on simple measures such as allocating an existing clerk to the job on a part-time basis, establishing some of the procedures recom-

Table 1-2.   Informal and formal BI.

	Informal	Formal
Scope	narrow	broad
Cost	low	high
Coverage	sporadic	continual
Evaluation	no	yes
Demand	low	high
Supply	low	high
Targeting	no	yes
Sources	irregular	systematic
Centralization	low	high
Quality control	no	yes
Strategic view	limited	focused
User-orientation	limited	focused
Dissemination	ad hoc	systematic
Regularity	no	yes
Organization and control	loose	tight

mended in this book, and raising every employee's awareness to BI needs. Beyond this, a BI effort requires executives who can think straight on the subject. Interestingly enough, we have found that owners of small companies are natural BI collectors, and their companies are always on the alert for competitive data. But without organization, by which we mean a formal system, much BI effort is bound to be wasted.

Another misperception is that BI is a luxury, a staff function created in fat organizations with abundant resources, which has no relevance to the bottom line. Yet this was disproved in a study by two Canadian researchers (Miller and Freisen 1977, p. 269), who analyzed 81 detailed case studies of business organizations for the common profiles of successful corporations versus failing ones. They came up with ten "archetypes," six for successful and four for unsuccessful organizations, deduced from empirical findings on 31 variables. The study found that intelligence effort was one of the most important factors separating the successful from the unsuccessful organizations. In all but one of the successful archetypes, intelligence activity was judged by the researchers to be "sizeable," "concerted," or "substantial"; in the failing organizations, intelligence effort was described as "poor," "weak," and "lackluster." One statistical finding was that the highest intelligence score among the failure archetypes was lower than the lowest intelligence score among the successful archetypes. As the researchers put it: "The intelligence factor discriminates perfectly amongst failure and successful archetypes." Our experience concurs perfectly with their findings.

2

The BI System—An Overview

There are five distinct functions to any intelligence activity, whether it is carried out by John le Carré's Circus personnel, or by a business executive. These functions, taken together, constitute the BI system. They are:

1. Collection
2. Evaluation
3. Storage
4. Analysis
5. Dissemination

Figure 2–1, on page 18, presents a flowchart view of the BI process and its relation to the system's components (inside the large box labeled "Business Intelligence"). This chapter is an overview of the organization of the five BI system components. In other chapters we will discuss how to organize the five components and the problems encountered by companies that have implemented this system, present various organizational solutions, and offer advice about the most effective route, whenever our experience has indicated a superior approach to structuring and operating the system.

Management makes two kinds of decisions: strategic decisions with long-term impact, and tactical—operational—decisions that have immediate, short-term impact. The BI process starts when manage-

Figure 2-1. The business intelligence process.

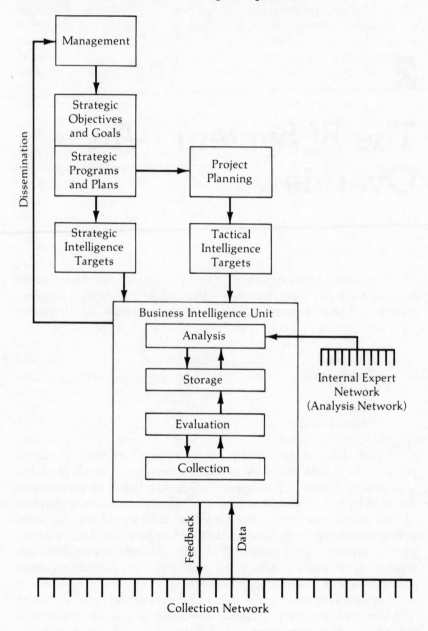

ment determines the strategic objectives of the corporation, from which strategic programs are developed. The strategic programs dictate certain strategic intelligence targets, as well as the priority of those targets. At the same time, projects that go into the project planning stage require tactical information (that is, short-run intelligence) for their execution. These two broad areas of decision making—the strategic and the tactical—direct the operation of the BI system. In the next two chapters we present a particular method for determining the targets for the BI system.

Our approach for setting targets for BI collection begins with the decisions made by managers and the informational support they need to make these decisions. These informational requirements are called critical intelligence needs. Since every executive will have his or her own unique information needs, the optimal way to target a BI system is through cooperative planning by the BI specialist and the manager-user. We propose a technique, termed the BI audit, that guides the BI specialist in assessing the BI needs of management.

The setting of targets for the BI system requires the assessment of critical intelligence needs specific to the company through the audit. There are, however, some common principles of strategy making that convey particular intelligence requirements regardless of the company, the industry in which it operates, or the system used. Not surprisingly, these principles are those on which the analysis component of the system is based. Competitive analysis is a specialty all unto itself. However, since it bears implications to setting targets for BI, we have included it in the separate chapter on critical intelligence needs.

For the next component of the system, collection, we present the internal collection network approach. The internal collection network (ICN) is the coordinated, motivated, and connected network of employees who access sources of information and report the data in a prescribed manner. The collectors, who are all the employees with potential BI data, should be trained and given incentives to perform collection activities. In the chapter on the ICN we present the accumulated experience of companies that have created and operated such a network. In the chapter on the intelligence audit we suggest some practical guidelines to the identification of potential collectors and the charting of communication channels in the organization that may serve as a basis for the transmission of BI data.

Raw data collected by the ICN must undergo some processing before they become information. This processing is what we term

evaluation. At this stage the data are evaluated for reliability, usefulness, and urgency of action required, among other factors. The
evaluation is not the same as analysis, because it is the technical, not
analytical, processing of data. Analysis consists of collating data,
condensing information, drawing conclusions, building scenarios,
studying implications for competitive positioning, and recommending action.[1] The BI system handles analysis with the help of internal
experts, analysis committees, and other organizational tools. We
devote a section in the chapter on organizational structure to discussing the experience of companies in the management of the analysis
stage.

Once the ICN collects and reports the data, and technical evaluation discards the unusable portion of the inflow, the issues of
storage and dissemination must be considered. The system approach
we advocate is not dependent on computerizing these functions, but
experience shows that this is where the future lies. Efficient storage
and dissemination are needed to ensure that data are easy to retrieve
for analysis, and that intelligence is disseminated to the right user at
the right time. The use of user interest profiles to match users with
intelligence, as well as the use of an effective recording/filing method,
will help to achieve these goals. The advances in technology in this
area make the computerized BI system, almost by necessity, the
preferred solution. We therefore devote substantial space to present-
ing the use of computers in BI.

Once the analyzed intelligence is disseminated to management,
the feedback loop in Figure 2–1 suggests that this intelligence may
have an effect on the strategy-formation process. Strategies sometimes change with the advent of critical intelligence, and proposals
rise and fall depending on the perception of environmental risks and
rewards. The result is a continual cycle of setting intelligence targets,
collecting and analyzing intelligence, and revising old targets.

The BI system is compatible with several different organizational
structures. Some big companies have instituted a separate BI unit,
while others house the system within an existing department. The
chapter on organizational structure presents the various organiza-

---

[1]The analysis of the information is a subject on which several books have
been written. Though we expound on it briefly in the chapter on critical
intelligence needs, we trust that our readers—if they are not already familiar
with the more popular works in the field, such as Michael Porter's (1980,
1985) books on strategy—will avail themselves of literature on the subject.
See also Rothschild (1984).

tional alternatives to BI design along with our favorite solutions. Throughout the book we will refer to the BI system and sometimes to the BI unit without in effect assuming that there is a separate unit. The system approach requires a center of responsibility for the coordinated operations of the five components, and as long as someone, somewhere, ensures this coordination, we feel justified in using the label, BI system (BIS).

A classic example for the operation of a BI system is a consumer products company that canceled a scheduled market test on the intelligence that a competitor intended to interrupt it with its own promotional campaign. Management then turned its BI effort to collecting intelligence on the rival's management objectives. It hoped to determine the rival's capability to engage in a sustained price war that management planned to bring about in a different market, as a retaliatory measure in case the competitor tried to interrupt a future market test. Since then, the fight between the two companies has become a famous case study in marketing strategy taught at every business school in the nation. The intensive role of BI in that war has been somewhat neglected.

The purpose of systematizing the BI process is to organize the activity to efficiently produce intelligence useful for decision making. Often management's problem is not the unavailability of data. Rather, the problem is too much of it and too little useful intelligence. As one manager put it: "We have a sea of data and a desert of intelligence." Many managers painfully realize that the amount of raw data confronting them is enormous. The number of business publications, on-line data bases, and other sources of data about the environment have been growing exponentially during the last decade. It should not be the task of the manager to collect, analyze, and digest this information. This is why a business intelligence system exists. The business intelligence system provides a method for information filtering that serves (1) to prevent information overload, and (2) to assure that what is important gets through to the user, while what is not important is filtered out early on.

Information filtering occurs at every stage of the BI process:

1. At the collection stage, the amount of data collected is limited by the specification of collection targets (see Figure 2–1). Collection targets assure that only what is needed for decision making is collected. The amount of raw data that the collector has to scan is reduced further by system procedures that identify which sources are most likely to provide the necessary data.

Figure 2–2.   How to bring vast amounts of data to a manageable
scale.

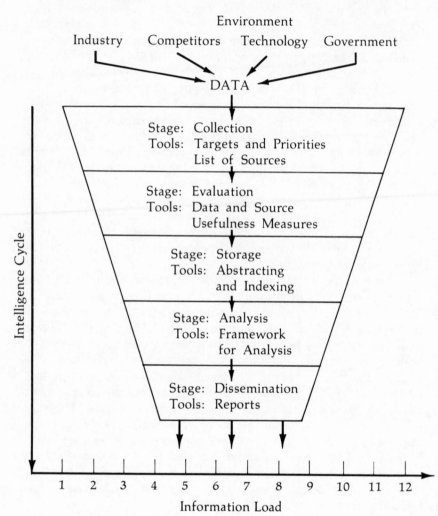

2. At the evaluation stage, unreliable data are discarded, and the remaining data are collated into information building blocks (IBBs).

3. When information is stored it is abstracted and categorized. It is thus packaged for easy scanning and access according to target and subject of interest.

4. At the analysis stage, information is collated and synthesized by imposing on it a framework for analysis. The result is intelligence that is presented to users in a highly organized and compact fashion and is directly relevant to user needs and readily usable. While the intelligence embodies all the information value existing in the original data, in itself it represents only a small portion of the vast amount of the original data.

5. Finally, the BI system includes procedures for efficient dissemination of intelligence. This assures that users receive the intelligence they need to support their business decisions while at the same time preventing useless information from cluttering their in baskets.

Figure 2–2 describes the information filtering characteristics of the BI system with a hypothetical scale for information load on the horizontal axis. Filtering is vital because management is flooded with *data* but starves for *intelligence*. If you share this belief you will find the rest of the book helpful in setting up a better BI system.

The remainder of the book is devoted to a detailed description of the BI system. Each function of the system will be discussed as to its design, control, and implementation in various organizational settings. Problems and pitfalls one may encounter during the implementation of a BI system will be pointed out and ways to overcome them will be discussed.

3

Setting Targets for the BI Program

The goal of the intelligence program is to supply decision-makers with information to serve as a basis for their decisions. As such, the program has to be geared to the kinds of decisions that take place within the organization. There are many levels of planning within an organization, and therefore many kinds of decisions that take place. The task of the business intelligence expert at this juncture is to identify what role each hierarchical level plays in shaping the corporate and business strategy, which issues are therefore of concern to each level, and finally, what information would be useful to each level.

It is important to distinguish among the various planning processes that take place in the organization. This is necessary to decide where in the organization to locate the business intelligence function, whether the company should have one corporate function to serve the total organization, whether each business unit should conduct its own business intelligence operations, and whether the function should be broken down along product lines. As will be demonstrated in the chapter on organizational structure, the design of the BI function has an important bearing on the smooth operation of the BI program.

Once the information requirements for each level of decision making are identified, it is possible not only to establish what intelligence should be disseminated to each area within the organization, but even before that, to determine what information should be collected.

The levels of planning within the organization that should be considered, and the management information needs for each, are:

Corporate level.   The function of the corporate level is to establish the goals of the firm, state corporate objectives, and define corporate philosophy and values. It is also the function of this level to recognize worldwide technical and market trends, and define the long-term domain in which the company will compete. This level also plans the allocation of resources to the company's business units and coordinates the sharing of resources among them.

Group level.   Companies set up a hierarchical organization called "the group" to plan how technologies will be shared among a number of business units or to coordinate the activities of business units in meeting the needs of a common group of customers.

Business unit level.   Business units are defined by their product, markets, or delivery system. Most of the strategic planning effort is done at the business unit level.

Product level.   Typically, this is where products, prices, sales, and services are planned.

These organizational hierarchies require both strategic and tactical information. Of course, at the highest level, the corporate level, the requirement is mostly for strategic information, while the lowest organizational level is the greatest consumer of tactical information. At this point management will need to know if there is, in fact, any difference between the intelligence required for strategic decisions and that required for operational decisions. The issue is important, for if strategic and tactical intelligence require different inputs and analysis, we may be able to separate our BI system into two distinct processes serving different needs. In general, strategic decisions require a broader monitoring of the environment, and must be sensitive to evolving customer, social, political, regulatory, demographic, and technological trends. Operational decisions require concentrating on the current business environment, especially competitor, customer, and market conditions. We find, however, that many pieces of intelligence collected for the formulating of operational decisions can contribute greatly to the broader puzzle required for strategic moves. Thus, intelligence on current policies of competitors will be used to develop a competitor response profile that will be a part of any strategic proposal. An interesting example is of a company that assiduously collected information about price changes in the competitor product line, which consisted of several thousand different items. Price changes were used by the sales force to promote its sales activities. At the same time a computer model was developed to track the pattern in price changes. After a sufficient amount of information was collected, the model was run and yielded an interesting picture of the competitor's price movements, which on the surface seemed patternless. It appeared that the competitor had gradually been changing the price structure—and thus the positioning—of the whole product line. It also became obvious that because of price changes the margins on the various products had changed, and that the competitor was emphasizing the low volume, high price end of the product line, a departure from its historical strategy. The point is that tactical information analyzed in a particular way revealed a change in strategy and therefore was important for strategic intelligence as well.

Critical Intelligence Needs

As discussed above, different levels in the organization will have different information needs, depending on the decisions made in that level. These information needs are called critical intelligence needs (CINs). Thus, for decisions made at the corporate level, CINs may include the general health of the industrial sectors relevant to the businesses of the corporation, the economic, political, technological, and social climates that affect the corporation, emerging technologies and the threats and opportunities they create for the firm, and even global trends in primary markets.

The decisions to introduce a new product will involve a different set of CINs. Here are some examples of critical intelligence needs for decisions relating to the introduction of a new product:

1. Existing competing products
2. Announced product introductions by competitors
3. Products on competitors' drawing board

4. Competitors' ability and range of immediate response to product
5. Competitors' ability and range of response in 1–2 years
6. Likelihood and strength of competitor response
7. Potential national or international competition from outside the industry
8. Potential market share
9. Industry growth or stability
10. Barriers to entry
11. Availability of materials
12. Availability of distribution channels
13. Government response

A thorough discussion of critical intelligence needs appears in a later chapter.

Often CINs have to be assigned an order of priority, simply because the business intelligence program may not have the resources to cover promptly or with adequate depth every single need. The simplest method of establishing the order of CIN importance is to ask the contributors to the list of CINs to use a Likert scale (see below) to assign a number from 1 to 5; the number determines the importance of answering a given CIN:

1-----2-----3-----4-----5

not important   extremely important

Participants should consider the following factors in determining priority of CINs[1]:

- The expected impact on the company of the event to which the decision relates
- The speed with which the event could impact the company
- The time required by the company to implement the decision or to react to an event

If, for example, the target is a particular competitor, a CIN—such as, "What are the competitor's plans regarding capacity expan-

[1]Adapted from David B. Montgomery and Charles B. Weinberg, "Toward Strategic Intelligence Systems," *Journal of Marketing* (Vol. 43, Fall 1979), pp. 41–52.

sion?"—may receive a high priority in an industry in which capacity increases in large increments only, and it takes a long time to construct a plant, as in the steel industry. On the other hand, in an industry facing rapid technological change, a high priority will be assigned to CINs regarding new product development and a lower one to capacity changes.

As for the list of 13 CINs on pages 26–27, the executives of the company in which the list was compiled ranked "Government response" as the most important, followed by "Competitors' ability and range of response in 1–2 years." This ranking reflected the nature of the company's industry (pharmaceutical) in which government regulation is severe, and product development and testing take a long time.

The Process of Establishing CINs

In setting critical intelligence needs, it's essential to consider both strategic and tactical information requirements, as shown in Figure 3–1.

As the figure shows, the topics and objects of intelligence collection are a function of strategic and short run (tactical) planning. In other words, the purpose of a BI collection is to provide the information input that is needed by strategic planners and management at all levels of the hierarchy, and for the detailed planning of projects. It is therefore essential that managers at all planning levels, from top management to middle management, be involved in determining the broad classes of information they require (competitive, economic, social, political, technological, governmental), and the particular targets (existing competitors, potential competitors, government agencies, and others) about which intelligence information should be collected.

There are two techniques that can be used to identify intelligence targets. One is for the person in charge of setting up the BI system to review strategic objectives, goals, existing strategic plans, marketing plans, product strategy plans, and extract intelligence targets. With the other technique the person in charge of setting up the system can involve potential users from the entire organization in deciding upon the intelligence targets. Certainly, this can be done as part of the intelligence audit. (The audit will be discussed in a later chapter.) The idea is to make the system useful to major decision-makers in

Figure 3–1.   The process of setting targets.

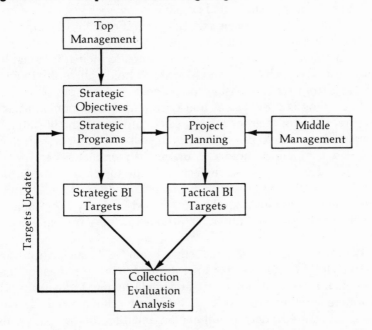

key areas—such as planning, business development, R&D, marketing, product management—and others, such as the CEO, who are
responsible for strategy formulation and execution. Their input is
crucial to obtain an accurate list of targets. Several methods that have
proved successful in extracting information on targets are provided
in the chapter on the audit. One advantage of compiling the list
through the audit is that you can achieve early on a high level of
consensus among executives. As a result, all the additional steps in
the process can be implemented more easily. In several corporations,
the final list was shaped at a major meeting of top management.
Thus, management involvement was assured at a very early stage.

     The basic idea behind developing the list of targets is the narrow-
ing down of broad categories of interest to specific topics. It should
always be kept in mind, however, that any list of targets may overly
restrict the collection of information. For a BI system to be effective,
it must be flexible. The flexibility is especially important in two areas:
1) urgent and unplanned requests for information that require special
intelligence inquiries, and 2) unstructured scanning of the environ-

ment to detect opportunities (offensive intelligence) outside the defined domain of the established targets.

Unstructured scanning is especially significant to companies that emphasize innovation, companies in fast-moving, high-tech areas, and companies involved in acquisitions outside their traditional line of business. For such firms, the BI system should allow the freedom to deviate from the established directions. An example of unstructured scanning is a BI system that encourages R&D personnel who read extensively in their technical areas to provide to the BI staff a list of emerging technologies that may impact the company. Indeed, farsighted companies could encourage their employees to try and detect social trends whose impact will extend far into the future. Thus, the monitoring of the official, sanctioned list of targets might be broadened through a kind of controlled curiosity. That spirit of controlled interest, we submit, is a hallmark of a true intelligence person.

We once observed an interesting example of such an attitude toward collections targets with an entrepreneur who published magazines in the areas of wholesale and retail foods. To keep up with consumers' preferences, social trends, and other market developments, this entrepreneur maintained a small food store on the first floor of his publications' headquarters. The store's employees were instructed to engage in conversations with the customers specifically for the purpose of collecting information. Though the store was only marginally profitable, the entrepreneur considered it a very important element in his operations.

It may turn out that a company will need to resort to outside help in certain cases, not only for obtaining the appropriate information, but also in learning to ask the right questions. Mergers and acquisitions, R&D decisions, and new business development are areas of strategic decisions that often involve new products, new industries, or new markets. Thus, they present novel situations where prior knowledge may not exist. The need for intelligence in making these decisions is self-evident: The firm typically has little knowledge outside its current domain and therefore must collect information on the new area. Such may be the case in identifying acquisition opportunities, selecting acquisition candidates, introducing new products, seeking a venture partner, or entering a new international market. That few, if any, managers in the corporation would be likely to have existing knowledge of the characteristics of the novel situation makes it the most difficult area in which to specify targets.

Flexibility can also be introduced into the list by periodically reexamining targets. The BI process is dependent on continual feedback, and an outdated target list is as good as last year's economic model. Though one does not need to go through the time-consuming process of another audit involving the entire managerial layer, it is imperative that in revamping the target list, major users of intelligence have a say in the process of reassessing the list of targets and their priorities.

Which Competitors to Follow

Any BI system should monitor existing competitors with particular targets listed by priority. Your company may only have a few competitors (in which case there is no problem in listing them) or many. For a diversified conglomerate, the problem of existing competitors is complicated by the fact that each subsidiary will have its own list of competitors and the corporation as a whole may have other competitors at the corporate level. We have talked to companies that had hundreds of product lines and faced dozens of competitors. When a BI system operates on the corporate level for the whole company, even if each subsidiary is instructed to develop and monitor its own list of competitors, it may be impossible to keep track of all those on the list. For that kind of centralized BI system, a method is needed to limit the list of competitors to be tracked. A simple method used to narrow the list of current competitors is to set a priority coverage for each competitor based on how important the division competing with it is to the corporation as a whole; or if it's a subsidiary, how important is a particular product line in which it is competing. In other words, whether targets are developed at the headquarters level (for a corporate BI system) or the subsidiary level, the trick is to decide on a cutoff point below which a competitor may be ignored. One such cutoff point that we used in a giant multi-subsidiary pharmaceutical company was based on the decision-grid in Figure 3–2.

On the vertical axis we listed the product lines of the corporation ranked by the importance to the overall performance of the company. The particular technique we used was to multiply the percentage of total corporate profit contributed by the product line by the five-year

Figure 3-2. Who are your current competitors?

Your company may have only a few competitors, or many. In addition, your company may be diversified into a variety of product areas, with competitors unique to each area. If you have many product lines and many competitors, you may not be able to thoroughly cover every competitor. In order to achieve a useful competitor list, ask your managers in the various divisions to submit a list of companies they consider as the major competitors in their product areas and companies who, while they currently are only minor competitors, can become major competitors in the near future.

The next step in defining a list of competitors about whom you collect intelligence information requires setting priority coverage for each competitor, depending on how important a certain division or product lines is for the corporation as a whole. The following decision-grid serves as a useful tool for this task. The grid consists of a list of competitors ranked by their market share on the horizontal axis and by your product lines on the vertical axis, where product lines are ranked by their contribution to overall profits multiplied by projected growth rate for the product.

| | % of Total Profit | Competing Company Market Share X Expected Growth Rate | | | |
Product X Expected Growth Rate	1.0	.8	.6	.4	.2
A		Co. M			
B			Co. P		
C					
D					
E				Co. R	
F					Co. Q
G					

average of its expected growth rate. Thus, if product line X contributed 30 percent of the corporate profit and its expected five-year average growth rate was 20 percent, this product line received a score of 30 × 20 = 600. Product lines were then ranked by their total scores.

On the horizontal axis we ranked current competitors, by product line, according to their importance. The formula we used was to take each competitor's current market share for that product and multiply it by the following year's growth rate in that market share plus 1. Thus, for product F in the grid, competitor Q had 20 percent of the market and was expected to remain at that level for next year, so we assigned the score of .20 × 1 = .20. The competitors were then ranked horizontally by their score, with the most threatening competitor on the left.

If expected growth in market share is unknown, one can use other indicators of competitor importance, such as expected growth in sales or earnings for that product line. While accurate data may be hard to obtain, the purpose of the exercise is to make a qualitative judgment, not a quantitative forecast. Therefore, one may simply decide to use available data of, say, the market share alone, or even subjective estimates of the degree of threat posed by each competitor. The reason we prefer to use a more complicated formula that includes both current state (market share) and future indicator (expected growth) is to account for currently small competitors that may be expected to cause a much greater threat (perhaps due to a new product) in the future.

As an additional method, one may ask several managers from various departments or functional areas to develop a list of the most important competitors. The comparison of the answers is sometimes as illuminating as the final list itself, as it shows the different intelligence needs of different users. Overall, though, there is usually some agreement as to the several most important competitors.

A special topic for BI collection is that of potential competition. As Harvard economist Michael Porter (1980) emphasizes in his book *Competitive Strategy*, competitive strategy involves the consideration of the threat of entry by potential competition. In terms of a BI target, the threat of potential entry is rather an ambiguous target for collection. Nonetheless, collectors should be instructed about the interest of top management in the subject. One way the topic can be included in BI collection is to specify, as a CIN, the plans of customers and suppliers to integrate backward/forward. Another method to assure monitoring potential entry is to assign a collector to look specifically for indicators that firms for whom there is an obvious strategic advantage to be in the industry are on the acquisition trail. Obviously there is no guarantee that such general scanning will forewarn management of the plans of a company to enter the industry, especially if entry is part of a diversification strategy of the unrelated-business type. One should always keep in mind that defensive intelligence (of which this target is a clear example) is always more difficult to conduct than offensive intelligence since the target does not usually announce its plans well in advance. Nevertheless, general scanning for possible entry is worthwhile, especially for small innovative firms with new products. An example of a BI failure in that particular area that led to company failure is the case of EMI, the British company that developed the first medical scanner in 1973 and eventually had to be sold out at a loss because management did not pay close enough attention to entry into that industry, and the rapid satiation of the market that followed. Thus, despite the difficulty in monitoring potential entry, it should be a BI target for every company whose market is not securely blocked.

Final Word

Companies have developed "war rooms," their walls covered with matrices with colorful circles representing the competitive positioning of rival firms. These matrices are constantly updated to reflect changes in market shares, growth rates, and other strategic success factors. It will not be unreasonable to suggest that one wall be reserved to display a list of intelligence targets and a summary of accumulated intelligence reported on them. Periodically, this matrix can be updated to keep the BI staff alerted to changes in targets and areas in need of better coverage. In addition, the accumulation of information in particular cells of the matrix can alert the staff to the emergence of a meaningful intelligence picture. Such displays are popular among intelligence professionals and they should prove useful in corporate offices as well.

4

Critical Intelligence Needs

What intelligence do managers need to help them make business decisions? This is a straightforward question and it might seem that the answer is simple, too. Thus, the typical assumption of management books and guides is that managers know what information they need to make good decisions. It is assumed that when it comes to information to support their decisions, executives know exactly what they need. Therefore what might prevent managers from making the optimal decisions is a paucity of the right intelligence.

Our experience during audit after audit, as we interviewed managers for the kind of information they needed to make their decisions, showed otherwise. Contrary to the textbook description of managerial decision making, information input is an ambiguous issue for the majority of executives.

It is a difficult task to clearly formulate one's information needs. It is easier to make decisions based upon whatever information is available at the moment, without articulating information needs or investing a great deal of effort in collecting and analyzing the appropriate data. Executives adapt quickly to information-poor environments, where decisions are made without the proper intelligence background. Unfortunately, this often leads to decisions that are made based upon invalid assumptions or superficial intelligence. At the same time, if offered information these managers will ask for much more than they need, exactly because they are unclear about their objectives for receiving the information. Hence, faced with large quantities of information they may not be relevant to the task at hand or that they cannot relate to the business decisions they are to make, they dismiss the business intelligence effort as useless and wasteful.

It is also not uncommon to find companies whose business intelligence system generates comprehensive competitor profiles that all too often look like a laundry list of the competitor resources (e.g., production facilities, sales force, product line, advertising expenditures, etc.). Decision makers who then receive those thorough profiles may not readily know how to use them in their decision-making process.

The purpose of this chapter is to aid managers in integrating business intelligence into decision making. It deals with the intelligence required for particular decision areas. While each situation may call for unique information input, there are some common information building blocks underlying specific competitive decisions. We review a sample of these in the following pages.

It is suggested that the executive, using the following CINs as examples, and perhaps with the help of the BI information specialist, explore the information needs related to particular decisions. Such questions should be answered as: What specific decisions need intelligence input? What kind of intelligence is needed? What intelligence is absolutely necessary and what intelligence is dispensable?

Decision Types and Intelligence Requirements

Every major business decision requires intelligence input. Some executives learn this fact the hard way: A merger that doesn't work, a new product that arrives too late on the market, entry into a market that evokes fierce retaliation, or capacity expansion that is matched and leads to chronic overcapacity in the industry.

As a general rule, no major business decision should be undertaken without serious intelligence backup. True, some decision areas require more input from the BI system than others, either because the benefits of good intelligence are greater than elsewhere (as in mergers and acquisitions), or the problem is decidedly more complex (as is the case in strategic planning). We can safely say that no decision area should be neglected, and all should be supported in some way by the BI system.

Once said, the reader should keep in mind that we do not assert that all strategic decisions can succeed if only backed by appropriate intelligence: Some strategies are better than others, regardless of the intelligence collection and assessment preceding their implementation. Then, too, a company may implement a strategy poorly, despite good intelligence and strategy planning. Finally, certain decisions will take place without the benefit of extensive intelligence simply because it may not be possible to get the appropriate information. Examples of this include those decisions that relate to unchartered markets, those that require knowledge of a rival's trade secrets, or those that call for forecasting the irrational response of a management team.

There are two general types of decisions made within the firm: operational decisions and strategic decisions. The former are the day-to-day decisions, the latter are decisions expected to have a long-term impact on the firm. Within this classification, the following areas of decision making require thorough intelligence input:

Operational Decisions

Arbitrage opportunities
Market threats

Strategic Decisions

Strategic planning
New product introduction
New business/new ventures
R&D decisions
Mergers and acquisitions
Capacity expansion

Operational Decisions

In day-to-day decisions, intelligence on current market conditions is a vital element. Every manager collects and uses such intelligence in the course of the day, in his or her areas of decision responsibility. In a typical working day, a sales manager collects and uses intelligence on customers, competitor pricing, promotions, and dozens of other relevant aspects of the market. Roughly speaking, two areas of intelligence are paid close attention: arbitrage opportunities and market threats. Arbitrage refers to immediate opportunities for profit—what economists call disequilibrium conditions. A cheaper supplier, a possible lead on a new account, or the resignation of an executive at the competitor are a few examples. Financial institutions, especially the big investment houses, are noted for their extensive, tactical intelligence-gathering networks that are targeted at immediate arbitrage opportunities. Trading companies are also heavy collectors and users of tactical intelligence for market opportunities.

Market threats refer to tactical intelligence on competitors' actions that might affect business. Examples of such actions include changes in pricing, hiring away of professional or executive talent, preferential treatment by distributors, changes in advertising themes, market tests, promotional campaigns, and penetration of imports. Other threats include adverse developments in market conditions, such as political developments, bankruptcies, changes in financing possibilities, supplier credit terms, and wage rates. In a typical corporation, tactical intelligence collected on these aspects of the business environment compose the bulk of intelligence flow.

Strategic Decisions

The forging of long-term objectives and strategies to guide the corporation, its divisions and subsidiaries, requires intelligence. Whether strategic planning is performed by the CEO, by line management, or as a formal staff function within a planning department, the formulation of long-term strategies requires the use of specific knowledge about the external environment. There are definite stages of the strategic planning process that call for BI input. To borrow the planning framework of Thomas Naylor (1980, Chapter 6) the formulation of strategies at the corporate, division, and department levels usually involves the following activities:

Review of the external environment
Assessment of the situation
Formulation of objectives and goals
Formulation of strategies
Derivation of project plans
Specification of operating plans
    Implementation and control

The first activity is the review of the firm's external environment. Naylor, Vernon, and Wertz (1983, Chapter 11) identify at least six different areas in the environment that the company should closely monitor to ensure that the strategy developed is viable. These areas are the economic environment, the competitive environment, the regulatory and political environment, the technological environment, the factor supply environment, and the social and international environments.

To track the macroeconomic environment, companies monitor growth, inflation, and future interest rates. None of these factors can be predicted with any degree of accuracy and, indeed, economic intelligence is the least reliable of all the intelligence input that goes into the strategic plan.

Monitoring the competitive environment is a necessary ingredient in strategy development since a strategy requires realistic assumptions about the behavior of competitors, and their reaction to strategic moves by the firm.

Keeping track of the regulatory environment includes the monitoring of pending legislation, changes in regulations, and the development of public pressures. For years the most pressing strategic issue facing the automobile industry, for example, was how to meet pollution control regulation, and strategic plans had to be organized around the best strategy to do so. The pharmaceutical industry is another example of an industry where tougher government controls forced a whole new approach to strategy and planning.

The technological environment is especially important for the strategies of high-technology companies, but also to utilities and even labor-intensive industries such as the textile industry. The revival of that industry in the U.S., despite what some saw as a fatal blow from imports, is attributable, to a large extent, to the streamlining of production processes with advanced technology.

The factor supply environment is not always at the top of monitoring priorities, but to prepare a strategic plan in the late 70s required some heroic assumptions about energy supply and the prices of raw material. Preparing for alternative suppliers is a common precaution in a well-developed strategic plan.

The social and international environments are clearly of relevance to the strategy formation of multinational companies, companies in controversial fields (cigarettes, weapon systems, drugs), and innovative firms looking to capitalize on fashionable trends (fashion, jewelry) or on foreign markets.

There is a need to monitor all of these areas to ensure that the strategic plan, whether it is a formal written document or not, is firmly grounded in reality and reflects more than the mere wishful thinking of management.

The intelligence collected in the first stage serves the second stage of the strategic planning process, the assessment of the situation by management, both at the business unit level as well as at the corporate level. Assessment refers to the evaluation of key success factors. The assessment will point to the opportunities and problems in the environment. Those will generally be in the areas where the firm must do well to succeed. Each industry will have its set of key success factors, and these factors may vary over time. Examples of success factors are market share, experience (in electronic manufacturing), good public image (in the financial institutions industry), especially skilled personnel (in the bioengineering research industry), low-cost production, breadth of product line, secured low-cost materials, choice locations (in the convenience food industry), patents, and efficient distribution system (in the beer industry). Thus, the purpose of the data collected by the BI personnel is to enable the decision-maker to arrive at an assessment of the situation faced by the corporation in terms of its position vis-à-vis the key success factors in the industry. The resulting opportunities and problems shape the rest of the planning process, from setting the firm's objective to choosing particular strategies. It is clear that the birth of a strategy, be it a marketing, diversification, or production strategy, at the subsidiary, division, or corporate level, follows logically and chronologically the assessment of the situation, which, in turn, is based on the environmental intelligence picture provided by the BI program. It will come as no surprise, therefore, that the poorer that input, the poorer the resulting strategy.

Following is a discussion of specific strategic decisions. For each decision we outline the critical intelligence needs (CINs). Critical intelligence is a list of all the information categories pertinent supporting a particular decision. The reader should be cautioned, however, that while it is possible to create a comprehensive CIN list for every decision, in reality there are both time and budget constraints on the ability to obtain information and analyze it. One should therefore consider that not all CINs relating to a particular decision have equal importance and that time and effort should be spent on collecting information (a) on the more important CINs, and (b) on those CINS for which information is more readily available.

New Product Introduction

The intelligence input required for decisions regarding new products is somewhat similar to that required for entry into a new business, since both decisions deal with the uncertainty of competitors' response and the barriers to intrusion into a new or existing market. The CINs we identified for this decision area are:

- What are the existing competing products?
- Have competitors announced new introductions?
- What products are on the competitors' drawing boards?
- What is the ability of competitors to respond immediately to the product? What defensive strategies had they employed in the past?
- Are competitors likely to try and disrupt market testing?
- Are competitors likely to "leapfrog" by introducing a new product in the middle of your firm's product introduction?
- Are competitors capable of blocking distribution channels for a new product that is to be distributed through channels other than the firm's traditional ones?
- Is the availability of raw material supplies to the new product guaranteed? Are suppliers vulnerable to competitive pressure from your rivals?
- What is the ability of competitors to respond in the longer run? How would they be likely to respond?
- What is the potential competition to the new product from foreign firms? From substitutes? Can one expect joint ventures or defensive coalitions against the new product?
- What regulatory response might be expected?

Entry into New Business

In considering the CINs required for a decision on whether to enter a new business, one should recognize that to reach a positive decision the return on investment in the new business should be larger than the corporation's hurdle rate. The return on investment in a new business depends on the following factors, which should serve as the CINs for a decision to enter: (1) the cost of entering the new market, and (2) the cost of operating once the firm is in the new business.

The first factor, the cost of entering, requires knowledge of the economics of the industry. The question is: How expensive is it to establish a foothold in the industry? If the incumbents have created barriers to entry, the cost of entry will be high. Barriers to entry take many forms: established brand names; economies of scale in production, sales, service, and so forth; proprietary technology protecting incumbent firms; distribution outlets tied up by incumbents.

The second factor refers to the expected competition once operations are established. This requires some medium-term forecasting of the strategies that incumbents will employ. To understand the possible response of incumbents to the new entrant, it is most important to gather intelligence on the incumbents' management, their motivation to fight the newcomer, their history of fighting entry, and their repertoire of offensive moves.

Entry into a new business means that the company is attempting, through internal development, to expand into a new market in which it may have little experience and expertise. Lacking substantial knowledge or access to intelligence about industries outside its current domain, your company may be forced to hire a research company with expertise in the new industry to do a market/competitive study. Even if intelligence is bought from the outside to support decisions to enter an unfamiliar new business, management should become familiar with the CINs for this type of decision. This will enable them to pose the appropriate questions to the outside research firm, interpret the information, and incorporate it into sound strategies.

Capacity Expansion

In deciding whether to expand production capacity, four elements should be investigated and they serve as the basis for the CINs: (1) *Expected future demand for the product.* When assessing expected future demand, the existence of substitutes and the possible change in their attractiveness vis-à-vis your own product should not be overlooked. (2) *Expected change in production technology.* This is obvious. It may be better to wait until the new production technology is perfected because it may yield a lower cost process, and/or a better quality product. The new technology may also increase or decrease the minimum efficient production scale, thereby changing the parameters of the decision. Thus, the firm may be forced to expand production by a larger degree than warranted by demand expectations, if there is an increase in scale, or, if there is a decrease, it may be able to proceed more cautiously with a small capacity addition. (3) *Expected capacity additions by current competitors or capacity build-up by potential new entrants.* To forecast additions to industry capacity you should understand the competitor's expectations about the demand conditions in the industry; its stake in the industry; its ability to add capacity (e.g., availability of cash). (4) *The cost of being left with access capacity.* This cost relates to the size of the investment, the life of the investment, and the ability to abandon it at minimum cost, such as switching production facilities to a different product line or selling off the assets.

Mergers and Acquisitions

Business intelligence for acquisitions is an area that has been especially overlooked. A large percentage of acquisitions fail, either because the performance of the acquired company does not meet prior expectations or because it fails to be properly integrated into the acquiring company.

The implication is that proper assessment of the characteristics of the acquisition target is of high importance. Whether strategic fit is a significant factor or not may be debated by theoreticians, but that an acquiring company should get the inside story on the target is undebatable. It is surprising how many companies do not get the right information, and nevertheless go ahead with huge acquisitions. The number of legal suits alleging misrepresentation brought against the management of acquired firms indicates some of the problems acquiring companies face in collecting reliable intelligence. In the case of a hostile bid, no legal recourse is possible, and it is exactly in these cases that finding out the intentions of the target can be of crucial value.

By the same token, it is not surprising that in several corporations with which we dealt, the BI system was first introduced by the initiative of the staff of the business development department or the department in charge of mergers and acquisitions. This was so simply because the awareness of the business development staff to the value of systematic BI was higher than that of others in the organization, often as a result of disastrous prior decisions that lacked good intelligence to support them.

The type of intelligence required by the M&A function is not much different than that required for industry and competitor analyses. The analyst is performing both analyses in the process of identifying an attractive industry, and a potential candidate within the industry.

Ebeling and Doorley (1983) outline five elements in the acquisition process:

Stating the firm's strategy
Developing acquisition criteria
Screening out inappropriate sectors
Reviewing favorable sectors
Zeroing in on target companies

This approach emphasizes the importance of strategic considerations rather than financial criteria in selecting the acquisition target. The objective is to identify a promising company in a promising industry. This is what Ebeling and Doorley call a "prime investment." A prime investment is an acquisition of a company where the acquirer has a high understanding of the activities of the target company, the external factors that pose a potential risk to the investment, and where the industry has high prospects.

In developing the acquisition criteria, management has to determine what it is looking for in an acquisition. If a clear statement of purpose is conveyed to the intelligence function, it is possible to at least give a broad direction to the scanning of the BI staff, and the entire internal collection network. If one believes in the value of multiple scanners and serendipitous discoveries of acquisition opportunities, as contrasted with the concentrated efforts of a few M&A analysts alone, the acquisition criteria should be made available to a wide circle of employees.

There are multiple reasons for an acquisition and consequently, as Cooke (1986, Chapters 3, 8) outlines, multiple criteria selection. First, management may look for synergy, or a way in which the combined firm can increase in value over the sum total of the separate entities. Synergy may exist in any area of the combined entity, and therefore the scanning should look for synergy in the broad spectrum of activities, technologies, and skills. Other reasons for acquisition are to acquire market power, to sustain growth, to acquire particular assets, such as an access to raw material in a vertical integration, to acquire assets at a bargain price, or to lower risk through diversification. The different motives suggest different criteria for acquisition. Thus, if the company were looking to increase market share, its scanning would be in the same industry. If the company were looking for synergy, its scanning would largely remain close to its own expertise. Diversification calls for scanning for companies and industries with cash-flow patterns different from the acquirer's own pattern. Bargain, or speculative, acquisitions call for scanning for mismanaged companies and companies in trouble. In short, the acquisition policy's objectives will determine to a large extent the nature of the intelligence sought.

According to Ebeling and Doorley, the screening for promising sectors, as well as the elimination of unpromising ones, involves the use of the predetermined criteria for a scanning process. Once the obviously unsuitable sectors are eliminated, Ebeling and Doorley recommend screening for the promising sectors by investigating the industry trends and competitive dynamics. This involves the industry analysis discussed earlier. The scanner should first look for industries with favorable trends. This does not necessarily mean high growth, unless the acquisition criterion is growth oriented. Otherwise, an industry with sound prospects may be preferred by the acquirer. Cooke cites the example of a Swedish multinational firm that identified a demographic trend in the Swedish population where the percentage of older people could be expected to grow steadily over the next two decades. With that trend noted, the company has decided to develop its interests in the medical treatment area, through acquisition.

Next, the scanning should concentrate on identifying the critical success factors in the industry, and the position of the combined entity vis-à-vis these factors. Thus, the best target is the one that offers the best competitive position for the combined entity. Identifying the critical success factors, as well as the competitive position of the combined entity, requires the same type of data collection we discussed earlier in relation to Porter's five forces model, and his competitor analysis.

It is often recommended that an information checklist be kept to ensure that in investigating a potential acquisition candidate, all the relevant factors are considered. One such list is compiled by the accounting firm of Price Waterhouse and reproduced at the end of Cooke's book. The list is very similar to the one used in competitive analysis. Most of the difference rests with the fact that the data is assumed to be available through negotiation between the two merging firms. If the acquisition is a hostile takeover, or the inquiry is prenegotiation and therefore confidential, part of the data in the list becomes unavailable. Thus, it is doubtful that the acquirer can gain access to the target's unfulfilled contracts (item 46 on the Price Waterhouse list), or the exact method used in fixing selling prices (item 47) (Cooke 1986, pp. 258–259). Nevertheless, such lists definitely point to what intelligence is required for the decision in question and as such can serve to determine critical intelligence needs that will direct the BI program.

R&D Planning

Because the technological choices have broadened so much, R&D managers must make difficult decisions regarding the allocation of R&D funds for different projects. Companies find that to do this effectively, more information is required about markets and competitors. These CINs are relevant to R&D dollar allocations:

- Markets
    Size of the market targeted by the R&D project
    Substitute technologies and products
- Technologies
    Anticipated rate of change in the technology
    Maturity of the technology
- Competitors
    Others conducting similar research
    Their level of funding
    Competitor strengths and weaknesses in particular research areas
    How advanced their research is in each particular area
    Ability of competitor to translate research into products
- Critical success factors
    How to compete successfully in each technology

Other Uses of CINs

As noted earlier, forging the long-term strategy of the firm requires information about several domains in the company's business environment. One of them is intelligence about competitors and their strategic moves. Competitive analysis that culminates in the establishment of profiles for the major competitors provides information about the competitors' strengths and weaknesses, their likely future strategies, as well as an estimate of the competitors' responses to the firm's own change in strategy.

Competitive analysis is based on a theoretical framework of strategy formation and requires a solid knowledge of the elements of business policy. This is the subject of courses in business schools and outside the scope of a book on intelligence. For further information on competitive analysis the reader should refer to such works as Thompson (1985), Porter (1980, 1985), Fry and Killing (1986), or any other policy text. To complete the chapter, we will provide a short outline of competitive analysis from which CINs can be derived.

Competitive analysis includes the following elements:

1. Analysis of the competitor's strengths and weaknesses
2. Statement about its current strategy
3. Analysis of its management

Analysis of Strengths and Weaknesses

An analysis of the competitor's strengths and weaknesses is a basic ingredient of estimating its future strategy. In conducting the analysis, it may be useful to use an approach that Porter calls value chain, and Buaron (1980) and Bales et al. (1980) refer to as the business system concept. Both approaches advocate the dissecting of the firm's operation to a chain of value-creating components, and examining each component separately for competitive advantages or disadvantages. Buaron recommends analyzing the following components: the process technology, product design, raw materials, parts production, assembly, marketing, distribution, and service. Porter talks about a more complex concept, a chain of activities, from primary to support activities, that constitute the building blocks by which a firm creates its product and its value to the customer. Primary activities include: activities associated with providing the inputs to the product (inbound logistics); activities of transforming the inputs to the final product (operations); activities associated with moving the product to the customer (outbound logistics); activities associated with marketing and sales; and activities of an after-sale service. Porter (1985, Chapter 2) notes how support activities support each and every one of the primary activities as well as each other, and include human resource management, technology development (not to be confused with the narrower R&D function—technology development can occur in each of the primary activities, not only in manufacturing or product design), and procurement of inputs (from raw materials for the operations, to lab services for the technology development), as well as general administrative activities such as planning and financial control that support the entire chain. Analyzing each component or activity provides the means for identifying sources of competitive advantage, the strengths and weaknesses of the competitor.

The particular list one uses to size up the real capabilities of the competitor depends naturally on the purpose of the analysis. If the analysis is a comprehensive report on the competition—say a preparation of a competitor profile for the strategic plan—one may well use the list advocated by the textbooks. But, if the assessment of the rival's capabilities is done as part of a proposal for a particular strategic move, you may be better off using a list of factors (or functional areas) that are important to that move, and estimate the competitor's capabilities for response according to this tailored list. For example, in one case, the company was using its BI function to prepare better bids for government contracts. For each bid, the BI personnel were asked to provide intelligence about specific capabilities of the other bidders as related to the product/contract in question. This intelligence was then used to estimate the bid price the others could afford, and the suitability of their manufacturing, engineering, and management skills for the particular contract specifications. Thus, specific rather than general capabilities were more appropriate.

Current Strategy

Future strategy is probably related more to current strategy than to anything else, at least in the short run. As long as there are no radical changes in the leadership of the competitor, the inertia and economic dictates of the existing strategy will exercise a heavy influence on what the competitor is going to do next.

Charting a competitor's current strategy begins with the understanding of the various generic categories that seem to capture the essential features of this strategy. There are several levels of strategy (single/multiple business strategies, overall competitive strategy, and product market strategy, among others) and many variants of the basic strategies, which depend on circumstances in the business environment (such as a mature or a growing industry) as well as the firm's own competitive position (it may be an underdog or a leading firm). With so many books available to the reader, the list of possible strategies can end up as long as the entries for "Smith" in the phone book. We thus leave the extensive theoretical discussion to strategy textbooks. It is sufficient to say that firms compete by trying to build market share, maintain market share, or harvest their market position; that they do this by attempting to be a low-cost producer or a differentiated producer; and on the product-market level, they compete by serving either a single niche, multiple niches, or the mass market.[1]

In discussing the charting of the competitor's current strategy, it is important to look for signs that a major shift in strategy is about to take place. Referring again to Fry and Killing (1986), the following indicators are deemed useful:

Organizational change. A company replacing its top officer(s) may be headed for a new strategic direction, especially if the new executives in charge are not picked and nurtured by the previous top management. For example, the new management team at CBS, under Lawrence Tisch, may signify a more profit-oriented approach at the network. Similarly, acquisition may signal a change in policies if management styles differ at the acquiring and acquired firms, as was the case with Miller Beer after it was acquired by Philip Morris in 1970.

Change in capabilities. A competitor that is building strength by adding resources in a particular pattern may be signaling a change in strategy. Resources added in the manufacturing process, in either additional plants, new production technology, or additional process engineers, may point to an attempt to lower cost. On the other hand, the hiring of additional product engineers may point to an attempt to become more differentiated.

Change in input. A competitor changing suppliers, advertising agencies, or consultants may be trying to change strategy. The change might be in either direction: lower cost (if the new supplier is cheaper, or if the consultant is in the area of operation management),

---

[1]For a full discussion, see Fry and Killing (1986, Chapter 6). A reader interested in a summary description of the various combinations of strategy-industry-market position may wish to look at Thompson (1985, Chapter 16).

or a better differentiated product (if the new supply is of a higher quality, the agency is more aggressive, or the consultant is in product design).

Management

Management's beliefs, assumptions, and characteristic modes of reaction should figure prominently in competitor analysis. Beliefs together with goals and priorities, shape action. What the competitor believes about itself, its rivals, and the industry will determine what it thinks it can and should do. Thus, PEOPLExpress believed it could weather the competition in the busy North Atlantic market with low prices and low overhead. It couldn't and its beliefs about the response of its rivals proved wrong as well. Rolls Royce believed it could beat Pratt and Whitney and General Electric in the effort to build the best aero engine for the then developing mid- to large-size airplanes. That belief pushed Rolls Royce to commit beyond its capabilities, and to go into bankruptcy. Coleco believed it could overcome the technical problems with its Adam computer in the short time before the Christmas season, and therefore committed itself to large volume shipping before it even had a working model.

The Japanese counted quite heavily on the American automobile companies believing that the future belonged to the full-size car. It wasn't too difficult to find out about these beliefs: They were repeatedly and publicly expressed in speeches, annual reports, and interviews in the industry's trade papers. RCA never expected Sony and Matsushita to overcome so rapidly the price and technical barriers to developing a videocassette product as a substitute to its videodisc product. EMI, the developer of the medical scanner, believed it would take many years for future competitors to endanger its position. It took less than five. Beliefs about one's own capabilities, competitors' capabilities, and industry future, are clearly crucial in developing a strategy. It is possible to infer the beliefs, assumptions, and reactions of the competitor's management team by collecting intelligence about the personal and professional background of the executives. As an example, consider the claim made by management researchers Hayes and Abernathy (1980, pp. 67–77) that the tendency toward mergers and acquisitions exhibited by some top level executives could be explained by their legal and financial background. Another example is the change in strategy at Atari when its engineering-oriented founder Nolan Bushnell was replaced by the marketing executive, Raymond Kassar, when Warner Communications bought the company in 1976. The company ceased to be a leader in technology and became much more dependent on promotion, price competition with the growing competitive pressure, and marketing gimmicks. Perhaps this change could have been predicted by looking into the different backgrounds and experience of the two men.

Porter (1980, Chapter 3) suggests looking for past successes and failures that might have shaped management assumptions about how to compete. Fry and Killing (1986) suggest following the history of the competitor to identify a recurring theme in the competitor's past decisions that may point to a particular goal? For instance, the entrance of Kodak to the instant photography market was initiated with a relatively expensive product that could not have been expected to win a major share of the market away from Polaroid. Yet, Kodak's past history of emphasizing market share leadership in each one of its other markets should have suggested further product introductions aimed at the mass market, featuring unique qualities and low prices.

What the competitors believe are the capabilities, strengths and weaknesses, and strategic intentions of its main rivals. This question may be answered as part of the reverse competitive analysis technique (RCAT), in which the BI specialist attempts to ascertain what competitors think about his/her own company. Braniff International assumed that the major airlines would accept its maverick growth strategy or would be unwilling to risk a long battle. American Airlines moved to Dallas, Braniff's home base, and proved Braniff was wrong. IBM believed that its distributional and marketing strengths, as contrasted with those of Apple's, would get it its market share goal, despite the late entrance and less advanced technology it brought into the personal computers market. It was, of course, right. Apple did not find an appropriate answer to the giant's marketing muscle.

Not all managers are equally important in shaping the competitor's strategy. Fry and Killing (1986, Chapter 4) suggest the following questions to be asked in this connection: Who are the competitor's most influential managers? What drives them? Is the competitor a subsidiary where managers are put out to pasture? Is it a stepping stone to a successful corporate position?

The answers to all these questions, if puzzled together, piece by piece, should paint a relatively accurate picture of what drives the competition, and where it is driven to go.

Final Word

This chapter was devoted to examining the intelligence input dictated by managerial decisions. The assumption behind CINs is that without the necessary intelligence, business decisions (chiefly strategic ones) can not be made optimally. There are few studies that investigate the relationship of intelligence to decisions, and by implication, to company performance.

In a recent study that involved a simulated strategy game, Gilad and Roller (1987) examined this relationship in an experimental setting. Graduate business students were organized into eight teams (each team represented a firm and four firms comprised an industry) and competed within each industry by making up to 64 decisions per round in the areas of marketing, production, technology, and finance for a seven-round period.

In a variant on the original game, the researchers created a market for business intelligence in which firms could buy competitive information on other firms in their respective industry. Two experimental designs were employed. In one, the companies were told they had a fixed budget of $1.2 million annually for buying intelligence (the fixed-budget industry). The purpose of this design was to examine the type of intelligence bought rather than the amount spent.

In the second experiment (called the no-ceiling industry) no limit was put on spending. More than 200 items of intelligence could be bought at a fixed price, set high to prevent frivolous purchases. These items included competitors' product prices, sales volume, unit costs, sales expenses, advertising budget, investment in technology, and stock price.

Performance in the simulation game was measured using a weighted scheme of six criteria: profit, stock price, return on investment, assets, market share, and a measure of effectiveness of new investment. The result of the fixed-budget industry simulation showed that the purchase of marketing intelligence dominated, followed by cost and technology intelligence. More importantly, the trends in intelligence buying are of great interest. As the game progressed, firms based their intelligence purchase decisions mainly on the variables that affected performance significantly. This is equivalent to collecting BI according to critical success factors as discussed in this chapter.

Thus, when it became clear that the decisions of importance to winning the game were what pricing policy to follow and how much to invest in technology, such pertinent information as sales volume, price, unit cost, and competitors' investment in technology was purchased. It is clear from the results of the experiment that the team winning the game paid much closer attention to the intelligence relating to success factors than the losing teams.

In the no-ceiling industry the firm winning the strategy game outspent the closest rival by almost four to one. The higher outlays were not the result of simply having more cash to spend, since the winning team spent 12½ percent of its cash while the losing team spent only 1½ percent of its cash on intelligence. More importantly, the winning firm in this industry seems to have followed the same BI strategy as the winner in the fixed-budget industry. Buying intelligence selectively on identified critical success factors rather than spending equally on all categories of available information. Thus, the experiment found that winning firms spent more on intelligence than other firms and allocate their budget to information pertinent to critical success factors in the industry.

Our own experience shows that this holds true for real-world companies. There is a correlation between a firm's success and its competence at using intelligence critical to its decision making.

5

Establishing an Intelligence Collection Network

The heart of the business intelligence system consists of the internal intelligence network (IIN), which includes the internal collection network and the analysis network. The analysis network is composed of experts within the organization who interpret intelligence and give advice on matters relating to the competitor's operations, markets, the industry, and technologies. It may include experts on particular technical topics, particular markets, production technology, and product areas. (The analysis network is discussed at greater length in the chapter on organizational structure.)

A BI system will succeed or fail on the effectiveness of its networks. The network concept is not a novel idea. Every manager has his or her own "personal" intelligence network, the grapevine. The main problem with informal BI networks, which form spontaneously and are made of "circles" of collectors and end-users who feed each other with news and gossip, is their limited scope and coverage. These circles are composed of personal networks based on friendships, power bases, and departmental politics. To open up these circles and include them in a larger intelligence network is not an easy task. A collector feels more comfortable exchanging data with friends and close contacts in the organization rather than sending information to an impersonal BI center.

In this chapter we will describe the internal collection network (ICN), how to establish one, how to encourage everyone to participate in it, and how to manage it effectively.

What Is the ICN?

The internal collection network consists of employees who serve as collectors of intelligence information, especially field data. These employees are not sources of information per se. They are those individuals who access sources of information. A salesperson reporting a conversation with a customer about the competition is a collector; the customer is the source. Similarly, a new recruit who provides information about her previous employer during a recruiting interview is a source, while the interviewer is the collector. Thus, the ICN can be viewed as the eyes and ears of the organization, attuned to the business environment.

Putting together an accurate picture of the competitive situation is like playing a puzzle, and it requires that information be gleaned from many sources. It is also true that although the bulk of information comes from published sources, from trade magazines to on-line data bases, field sources of information provide the most recent, specific, directly relevant, and less widely known intelligence. Therefore, the goal of an effective business intelligence system—and of a successful ICN—is to tap as many field sources as possible.

In the course of doing business, executives and employees— indeed any person who has dealings with someone outside the company—acquire information informally through their close professional and personal associations. Engineers attend technical conferences where they meet engineers from competing companies. Purchasing agents talk daily to suppliers. Salespeople visit or call clients. Executives talk to their counterparts at the competition. All of them gain some competitive information. Unfortunately, the bulk of this type of competitive information is rarely passed along to those who can benefit from it most, except on a very casual basis.

The purpose of a formal ICN is to provide the structure and techniques to tap the abundance of competitive knowledge within the corporation. Members of the ICN are asked to perform the following tasks:

Identify and access sources of information
Collect data of interest to the BI establishment
Report information according to preestablished communication
    procedures
Participate in special, ad hoc intelligence projects

In case the ICN is also used to distribute the monitoring of published sources among members of the firm, the collectors will be asked to monitor certain publications, and to report—by abstracting, clipping, or other methods—items pertinent to a preestablished list of targets and CINs.

Though the tasks of the network may seem simple and straight-forward, they require a thorough job of organization, motivation, and education. The director of the ICN must be a diplomat, an expert, a charismatic leader, and a shrewd politician. It is his responsibility to see to it that a formal ICN is built on the following four elements:

1. *Information sources.* Identify what competitive information the various departments and individual employees possess. This can be done through the intelligence audit. (The audit is discussed in a later chapter).
2. *Communication.* Design the appropriate communication pro-cedures to regularly transmit data from collectors to users and/or to the BI unit.
3. *Motivation.* Establish a program of incentives to motivate employees to participate in the ICN and educate the organi-zation regarding the newly established program.
4. *Procedures.* Institute procedures to manage the collection process and provide feedback to the network.

Creating a network is not an easy task, but there are clear advantages to establishing an ICN over using a select group of BI personnel to perform the tasks of data collection. In companies that formed an ICN, it provided diversity in coverage of intelligence targets; it enabled the system to handle a larger quantity of data; the collectors provided expert screening of data; and an efficient network improved the timeliness of information.

Diversity and coverage. The network enables the system to access diverse sources of intelligence data, especially field sources. Because there are so many potential sources of intelligence information, the intelligence analyst does not have enough time to gather information from all sources. Even a well-staffed business intelligence unit, with several employees devoting their full time to the task, will find it very time-consuming to attempt to obtain information on an ongoing basis from all available sources. The ICN is necessary to cover all possible field intelligence sources even in an organization that has a large business intelligence unit and is adequately staffed. The reason for this is the nature of field information. Field information is rarely information that can be obtained through a formal interview. It is information that is passed on during whatever business interaction is taking place. Thus, an engineer may gain a bit of information from an engineer of a competing company while attending a conference. If, however, someone from the BI unit tried to call up an engineer at the competing company and ask specific questions, he or she would not get very far. Thus, the network enables the organization to access sources of intelligence that would otherwise be unavailable.

Quantity. The ICN allows the system to generate more data. A mature network operating at top capacity can consist of all of the organization's employees who have outside contacts. At a company like IBM, all employees serve as eyes and ears and combine into a widely spread intelligence network. Such a network can generate large quantities of data, by far larger than what a business intelligence unit can generate on its own. This is especially true for field intelligence, but, as will be shown later, may apply to published sources of information as well.

Screening. The ICN can be used to screen data by experts in the organization to determine appropriateness of immediate distribution of critical intelligence. Screening of incoming data by designated experts within the organization may increase the usefulness of data by enabling the right users to receive the information on a timely basis and thus enabling immediate response to events as they occur.

Timeliness. Use of the network improves the timeliness of information. First, rather than learning about events after they appear in the press or on television, the network provides a window on industry and competitive events as they occur, through the collection of field information. Second, the network provides ongoing scanning of the environment and therefore the earliest possible indications about changes. This is a great help to busy BI personnel who on their own may tap field information only intermittently—particularly when they are engaged in gathering information for a specific project—and may learn about the information much later.

For companies in rapidly changing industries, this is a crucial element. This was the reason why one biotech firm established a formal network early on when it was still relatively small. As the company's president noted, they could not afford missing out on competitive development—in this case, especially scientific development—because they were busy elsewhere. As he put it, in his industry, it could mean the difference between being very successful one day, and broke on the next. Even if this were an exaggerated statement, it would be closer to the truth than many executives realize. This particular president swore by the effectiveness of his network and its procedures for scanning and reporting. In less than three years, his company grew to be the fifth largest company in his industry and a leader in several product areas.

A different example shows how a delayed reaction can bring about a missed opportunity. At a large service company, a field representative reported an internal management struggle in a small, but profitable, entrepreneurial firm that was among his clients. The report came to the attention of the executive in a roundabout way, about three weeks after it was filed with the district sales manager, and only by accident. The executive immediately realized that the situation there represented an excellent opportunity for an acquisition, of which neither the "collector" nor his district manager had any understanding. By the time he got to call the firm, control had already passed to the founder's son, who, unlike his father, had no intention to sell. In the words of this executive, "I cried for days. It was such a perfect little acquisition for us, exactly what we were looking for. I could have killed the district manager for not passing it on, but of course, it wasn't his fault. He couldn't have known the real meaning of the gossip."

Building the Internal Collection Network

The internal collection network should provide information from two types of sources: (1) the field, and (2) published sources. The principles for establishing a network to gather information from these two sources are similar and where they diverge, the differences will be pointed out. Suffice it to say that there is no substitute to gathering field information through the use of the ICN. On the other hand, the task of collecting data from published sources can be accomplished by intelligence experts within the BI unit or other information specialists.

The process of building the collection network requires two elements at the outset: (1) an understanding of the type of information that is needed, and (2) knowledge of the information to which people in the organization have access. The intelligence audit is designed to find out both. (The type of information needed is discussed in the chapter on setting targets.)

Following the audit, the next step should be the establishing of a collection committee. The collection committee serves as a forum for the various departments participating in the ICN to share ideas about potential sources of information, ways of gathering data, and problems in collecting and transmitting information. It should also be a forum where participants receive ongoing information about intelligence targets and priorities, and where BI staff can learn what information is available to ICN collectors. Participants in the collection committee should be representatives from functional departments, typically the person second in command within each department. As we will show later, these representatives will also have an active role in establishing communications channels, motivating the collectors, and managing the collection process within their departments.

When the intelligence audit results are analyzed, companies usually find that almost all functional areas have some useful intelligence information. Some departments will naturally be more heavily represented in the ICN, because their employees have more contacts outside the company and access to more important competitive information. But bear in mind that when the ICN is put into place, no functional area that can serve as a source of intelligence should be left out. Figure 5–1 represents our experience of the typical composition of potential members of the ICN. Of course, the actual composition will vary from company to company depending on the industries in which they do business, how they are structured, their size, and the availability of particular employees to participate as collectors. For example, the major source of field information for an insurance company may be its agents; for a financial institution, loan officers and branch managers may have the main access to field data. For

Figure 5–1.　Field information sources and collectors.

Sources	Collectors								
	Sales/ Marketing	Service	Purchasing	R & D	Treasury/ Finance	Personnel	Legal	Key Execs.	Manufac.
Customers	X	X						X	X
Suppliers of equipment			X					X	X
Suppliers of raw materials			X						X
Distributors	X	X						X	
Competitors	X							X	
Former employees						X			
Trade shows	X		X					X	X
Technical meetings				X					X
Credit agencies					X		X		
Government						X	X		
Securities analysts								X	
Courts							X		
Consultants	X			X				X	X
Job candidates						X			
Trade associations	X			X				X	X
Subcontractors				X				X	X
Unions						X	X	X	
Regulators							X	X	

companies without a well-deployed sales force, as is the case in some service industries, technical representatives or customer-service engineers may possess the largest amount of BI.

Often it pays to be exhaustive and creative in establishing the role of various departments in the collection of information. No part of the organization should be overlooked. One midsize bank was concerned whether the competition had an inkling about the bank's new marketing concept and whether their competitors planned to follow similar lines. The bank's new plan called for a completely new positioning of the branch system and its services. This called for, among other things, extensive renovation to their existing branches. Management wanted to know if competitors were planning to renovate their branches. After some thought regarding possible sources for this kind of information, management called on the bank's building department, which was responsible for choosing local contractors to carry out the renovation work. Naturally the department had extensive contacts with these suppliers. Conversations with suppliers revealed that one bank had been hiring contractors to carry out renovation work, but the work was routine and did not call for a complete change of the interior design of the competitor's branches. Thus, management's fears regarding the competition were put to rest.

The topic of recruiting collectors to the ICN leads almost inevitably to the question of whether to impose on busy salespeople the added task of intelligence collection. Among various collectors in the ICN, salespeople are probably the most important. Yet the issue of using salespeople as collectors poses many problems. One company achieved a spectacular success in obtaining intelligence data when it reserved 30 percent of sales commission for an intelligence project. Conversely, we have encountered a top executive who, after an intensive full-day seminar on the design of a BI system, declared that his major problem was to get salespeople in his company to cooperate, and he could not see the system working until that problem was resolved.

Indeed, without the cooperation of the sales force, the ICN is without teeth. Unfortunately, there are some inherent problems in enlisting salespeople into the ICN. First, the primary objective of the sales force is to sell, not to gather data. The pressure to sell is high, especially in those companies facing intense competition—exactly those companies that need the BI system most. The salespeople of these companies need to be convinced that the additional task of gathering data is useful to both them and the company. Some incentive system is therefore a must.

Second, salespeople can always justify not filing business intelligence reports by claiming tight schedules with clients. It should be made clear by top management that they are expected to generate intelligence as a by-product of their sales efforts.

A major stumbling block to cooperation is that the sales management philosophy is at odds with the intelligence philosophy. Sales management philosophy stresses the establishment of as many new contacts as possible. Intelligence philosophy stresses the cultivation of sources through repeated contacts. Unless both philosophies are reconciled, salespeople will put intelligence collection low on their priority list. The fact that the two philosophies are at odds implies that an equilibrium must be struck, and it is the responsibility of top management to see to that. It is also recommended that the management of the BI function negotiate directly with the manager in charge of sales. A cordial relationship at this level can do wonders to improve intelligence collection by the sales force. One way to achieve such voluntary cooperation is to nominate the sales manager as a member of the intelligence committee.

Field information can only be obtained through the collection network. Published information, on the other hand, may be scanned by professional BI staff. Therefore, the role of the collection network in the scanning of published sources is less important and often is only an ancillary task. The BI department may informally ask managers and employees to keep their eyes peeled as they read technical journals or trade magazines for relevant information. Also, a formal system may be set up where particular people within the organization are assigned the task of scanning material that they are reading and to send relevant articles to the BI department. Sometimes the task of scanning publications is given to librarians in the business library. For scanning more specialized information, such as advances in product and process technology, scientists and engineers may be better suited for the job.

Establishing Appropriate Network Communication

The business intelligence process contains two conceptually distinct communication cycles, although in practice they may be interrelated.

One cycle involves the transmission of data and the other the distribution of intelligence to users. Figure 5–2 illustrates the two processes.

The function of the ICN is to collect data. The function of the business intelligence unit or intelligence specialist is to evaluate and analyze data and produce intelligence reports. On the surface it seems that the task of moving data from the ICN to the business intelligence unit is straightforward. In actuality, this is not so. First, existing patterns of data collection and distribution have to be taken into account when establishing a system. In most companies, the flow of intelligence has not yet reached the stage where the two communication cycles are separate, so you tend to find one cycle in which data is distributed along with intelligence to all users. In the transition to a formal BI system this has to be taken into account

Figure 5–2.   The cycles of data transmission and distribution of intelligence.

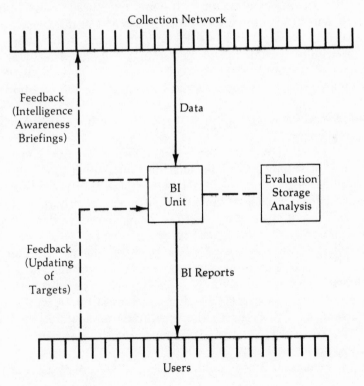

Collection Network

Feedback
(Intelligence
Awareness
Briefings)

Data

BI
Unit

Evaluation
Storage
Analysis

Feedback
(Updating
of
Targets)

BI Reports

Users

when restructuring communication. Second, in certain cases it is useful for some raw data to be circulated along with intelligence. For example, if managers are scanning the environment for new technological opportunities that are very broadly defined, they may need to receive a broad spectrum of technical and trade magazines through which they could browse. Last, some of the data that is collected should be distributed directly to users without further analysis. This is true in those instances where raw data has intelligence value on its own and may require immediate attention and action from final users.

Examples of raw data that may have immediate intelligence value are rumors of takeover plans by a competitor; field information about imminent price cuts by a competitor; information that a competitor is having serious problems in providing service to its clients; or field information that a competitor is planning to sell one of its plants.

The first issue that has to be resolved in regard to every item of data collected is whether it can be construed as a piece of intelligence in its raw form to be distributed immediately, or whether it is raw data to be accumulated for future use and reference. Unless all data are first sent to a central entity—such as a business intelligence unit or specialist, which then sorts the data according to whether they remain within the unit for future use or are routed directly to the end-user—the first question that collectors need to answer is: What constitutes intelligence, as opposed to data? Then the question becomes: Given that some collected data are intelligence, to whom should I send them, and, given that some things are just data, where would they be sent?

When establishing a communication system for data collection, the locus of responsibility for such decisions about dissemination must be decided on in advance. There are many means of communicating intelligence data: written intelligence reports, reporting via the telephone, voice messaging, electronic mail, recording data directly into a computer data base, and meetings. But before any of these "technologies" are established as the preferred means of communication, the general procedures for moving data and intelligence have to be established. Who is going to decide what data to collect, and when and where to send it? The individual collector? A local collection manager? The BI unit? The organizational solutions to these questions, as developed and experimented with by various companies, are presented below.

From an organizational point of view, there are three ways of structuring the data-reporting network: centralized distribution, decentralized distribution, and functional distribution.

Centralized Distribution

In this setup every piece of intelligence collected is sent to the BIU, and, in the absence of a separate unit, to the BI specialist within a designated department. (For convenience we will use the term BIU to refer to both arrangements.) Someone within the business intelligence unit decides whether the data should be put into a file for future use in conducting analysis or compiling reports, or should also be distributed to appropriate users. The distribution is determined by the BIU according to precompiled user interest profiles (UIPs), which list users' intelligence needs, supplemented by a suggested distribution list provided by the originator of the intelligence report. Centralized distribution is illustrated in Figure 5–3.

There are several advantages to centralized distribution:

Uniformity in distribution. The BIU maintains a comprehensive list of targets, priorities, and UIPs. Using the list of UIPs as the basis for distribution, the BIU ensures that all users get all the items relevant to their needs.

Cut down the amount of data distributed. Central distribution according to UIPs is an important step toward ensuring the distribution of intelligence as opposed to raw data. The intelligence specialists are supposed to integrate data from various collectors into intelligence reports and save executives from going over every piece of information that arrives through the network.

All relevant data are stored centrally. Because every item reaches the BIU, all relevant data will be sorted out and stored in the appropriate files maintained centrally, thus making the information available in one place. This is especially important in companies where individual employees are expected to plug into a centralized storage system for their own analysis, and it eliminates the familiar phenomenon of personal files held by various executives with valuable information that does not reach others who may need it. We have witnessed cases where the sales manager, for example, possessed critical field data in his files, but for political reasons these data never

Figure 5–3. Centralized distribution.

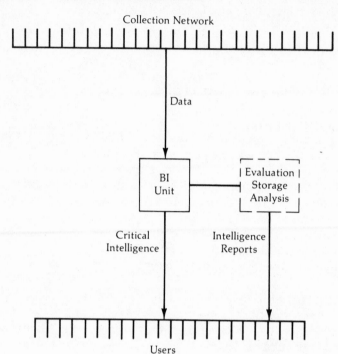

reached the other parts of the organization. The case is even worse with top management, such as the company president, whose collected data are usually relevant to almost every department in the company, but who are often too busy to share them with the appropriate personnel. A centralized distribution system solves most of these problems.

Unfortunately, there are also several problems with centralized communication. The following are the most frequently encountered:

Timeliness. Because intelligence reports are not sent directly, they will take longer to reach the ultimate consumers.

Volume. The ability to handle the distribution of intelligence reports centrally depends on the number of intelligence reports originated every day and the expected volume of intelligence reports as the BI system grows.

Expertise. Despite the availability of UIPs to guide distribution, the distribution of intelligence reports will be limited to some extent by the knowledge and expertise of the person in charge of distribution.

Some of these problems can be resolved by such technologies as electronic mail. These technologies will be discussed later in the chapter.

Decentralized Distribution

In a decentralized distribution system, each collector is responsible for the distribution of his or her data to the business intelligence unit *and* to the end-users (see Figure 5–4).

The advantages of the completely decentralized system stem from less bureaucratic interference:

Knowledge. Sometimes, the originator may be in a better position to know the significance of a particular item to certain users. This is typical in the case of extraordinary pieces of information that are not covered by the list of targets. It is also an advantage when strong personal networks exist.

Timeliness. The intelligence report is transmitted directly by the collector and avoids intermediaries.

All those who favor cutting down on paper should bear in mind that collectors will have to obtain and refer to a distribution list for every item they originate. Otherwise distribution will be limited to the number of people whom the collector knows personally to be interested in the data. This will defeat the purpose of a BI system, which is to improve the haphazard, uncoordinated activities of informal BI. Also, it may be difficult to keep collectors abreast of changes in needs. Further, this system makes it more difficult to control the amount of irrelevant data circulated through it.

A decentralized system can be improved by implementing the following:

Figure 5–4. Decentralized distribution.

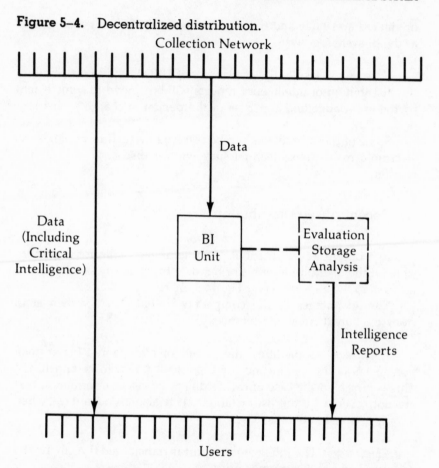

- Educate collectors about the company or the division in general, its structure, and the responsibilities of consumers of BI information. This can be done as part of the intelligence awareness briefings (see below).
- Educate collectors about user information needs and give them specific guidelines (UIPs) about who needs what.
- Provide them with feedback and updates regarding UIPs.

Functional Distribution

In this system, one person within each department or functional area is made responsible for the distribution of all material that is generated by the area. That person is charged with the task of determining whether an item is information that should be sent to the BI personnel only, or whether it is intelligence that needs action from some other department or executive within the organization. See Figure 5–5 for an illustration of functional distribution.

There are definite advantages:

Figure 5–5.   Functional distribution.

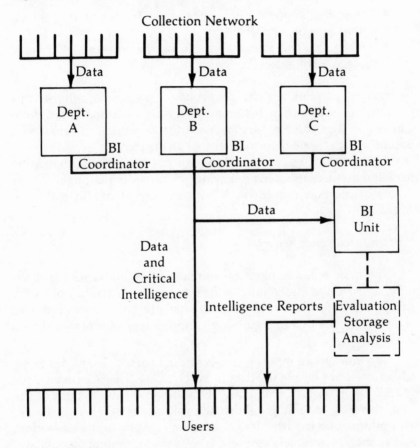

- Only one person within each area will have to be educated about the distribution process, user information needs, and changes in intelligence coverage.
- The person will have intimate knowledge of the information collected by his or her functional area and therefore will be able to disseminate the data with better understanding and insight into its significance.

But the disadvantages are these:

- The system imposes a disproportionate burden on one person within each department.
- Timeliness. The person responsible for dissemination may serve as a bottleneck for information flow.

Still, depending on the particular corporation's culture, this intermediate system may be the most workable solution to the problem of intelligence communities since the beginning of time: Who decides what is mere data and what is intelligence?

Given that an organizational solution to the communication issue has been decided upon, the following is a survey of existing methods of communication in various ICNs currently in use in corporate America.

Written Intelligence Reports

The basic building block of communication of the ICN is, typically, a specially designed intelligence report. An example of a written report format used by an industrial division of a medium-size company is provided in Figure 5–6. Another type of report is shown in Figure 5–7.

The intelligence report form shown in Figure 5–7 includes some additional items beside the data themselves, such as "Circumstances of Collection" and "Comments." In addition, at the bottom of the form there are several items that the collector is asked to evaluate. This information is particularly useful for assisting in dissemination, and so increasing timeliness, and is relevant for evaluating data and source. It is reasonable to suggest that data collected at a bar, for example, while the source was drinking, should receive a different evaluation score than data collected at a technical conference from a

Figure 5–6. Field intelligence report, sample A.

Report Date _____

Submitted By _____

Subject:

☐ Competitive   ☐ Product Quality
    Activity
                    ☐ Delivery

☐ Customer
    Activity   ☐ _____

☐ Product Performance

Date of Contact_____
Person(s) Contacted: Name(s) _____ _____
                      Company _____

Remarks:

☐ Information Only
☐ Action Required

Figure 5–7.   Field intelligence report, sample B.

Today's Date _____

Date Information Collected _____

Source _____

Collector _____

Circumstances of Collection _____

_____

_____

Content (please report what source said): _____

_____

_____

_____

_____

_____

Comments (your own reflections on the above): _____

_____

_____

_____

Data Usefulness: Data Reliability _____
                  Source Reliability _____
                  Timeliness _____

sober scientist. Thus, the circumstances of collection provide some clue as to the validity of the data.

The portion devoted to "Comments" on the form is also aimed at helping the evaluator. The separation of the verbatim account of the intelligence from the collector's opinion about its content intends to overcome the subjectivity of collectors who often tend to blend facts and interpretation. This form attempts to draw a line between the two, while at the same time drawing on the valuable knowledge and expertise the collector may have in interpreting the information.

There are two ways to set up a system of written intelligence reports (WIRs). One involves the creation of a completely separate WIR system. That means that special intelligence forms are designed—as per the above examples—and are used uniformly by the company-wide collection network. There is another way of establishing a WIR system. This system takes advantage of already existing channels of communication of information. Its purpose is to reduce the burden on collectors imposed by the need to write special reports. It also increases the likelihood that the reports will be written and transmitted to the BIU and users. Under this system, the WIR is added to other reports that collectors have to fill out for other purposes relating to their jobs. For example, at one company, quality assurance (QA) engineers visit potential suppliers for inspection of their production facilities. After such a visit they file a field report with the QA department. Often these suppliers also provide products and services to competitors so that competitive information is passed along at each visit. The WIR solution in this case was to add a tear-off page to the QA field report on which competitive data were singled out and that was sent to the BIU by the QA secretary. In another case an automotive supply company, facing increased competition, especially from newly arrived foreign competitors, began to put more emphasis on receiving up-to-date competitive information from the field through their extensive sales force. Ostensibly salespeople were supposed to report competitive information in their weekly call reports. In actuality, salespeople often failed to complete call reports properly with detailed information since they rarely completed them on time. Additionally, call report forms were designed in such a way that it was difficult to write down much information. The solution was to add to the call reports a special section that was to be filled out with competitive information and sent directly to the marketing department rather than the sales department. In this case the marketing department was charged with the task of tracking competitors.

Postcards

The postcard is a variation on the written report. At one insurance company, field representatives were given blank, pre-addressed postcards to be mailed with intelligence information from the field. The content of the postcard was brief, and if the information looked interesting it was followed up by a telephone call from the business intelligence unit for additional detail.

Telephone

To institute a written intelligence reporting system requires a great effort. People usually perceive the written intelligence report as a burden and unless there is a very strong drive toward instilling in collectors the need to fill out reports, the WIR system will operate sporadically. You may also find that within the same organization, some departments will take to the WIR system, while others will not. For example, a manufacturer of capital equipment established a business intelligence system with a collection network that encompassed every functional department. The WIR became the backbone of the system. Although most departments began to use the WIR forms, employees of the purchasing department would not. They did, however, occasionally call the business intelligence manager with competitive information. Finally the telephone communication method became the official method of communicating intelligence data from the purchasing department. This required someone within the business intelligence unit to take the calls and write down the information on the intelligence report form. To facilitate this process, the person assigned to this task recorded the incoming telephone intelligence messages on a microcomputer while listening to the information. The drawback to this method was that if the collector did not receive immediate response—that is, if the contact at the BIU was not there—there was a tendency not to call again and the information was lost.

Voice Message Center

A voice message center overcomes the drawbacks associated with the telephone method of communicating intelligence data. More and more companies are installing voice message centers, which are used for communication among busy executives, salespeople and their home office, and so on. The same system can just as effectively replace the WIR. But there are several caveats. First, on a written form, the collector is guided as to the ancillary information that is needed; in other words, clear instructions request information about the date the data were gathered, the source, and comments about the reliability of the source. By filling out the form, the collector is reminded to provide this information. In the phone communication method, the collector is prompted by an experienced BI person. In the voice message center message, there is nothing to remind the collector what information to leave. The report may therefore be incomplete, and may require someone from the BI unit to call back for clarification.

In addition, if there is no written report, someone has to listen to the incoming messages every day and transcribe the information for filing and dissemination.

Electronic Mail

The electronic mail system permits messages to be entered and delivered to a list of addresses. A set of UIPs, which contain key words describing the specific interest of the system's users, is maintained on the system and used to match users against incoming data and reports. In addition to the automatic addressing of data, the system can maintain a data base that includes current data messages available for scanning by any user. Any new message entering the system that meets the key-word criteria established by the user will automatically be put on that user's mail queue. The availability of current messages for scanning is especially valuable to users when they develop a new interest that is not reflected in their UIP.

There are many advantages to an electronic mail system. Among the most important is the automatic dissemination of information, which eliminates the problem of centralized or decentralized dissemination, since UIPs are centrally determined and updated but are available for any collector who enters a piece of information into the system for the creation of an immediate distribution list. Such a system, if available in every department and office in the company, including the sales force, can replace other means of communicating intelligence. It certainly can eliminate much paperwork.

Direct Computer Access

If the company maintains a mainframe-based on-line data base of competitive intelligence, information can be inputted directly into the data base through terminals throughout the company, including remote locations. Because direct inputting into the computer poses problems of control of the data and security, many companies that do have such systems have chosen not to use the remote input capability. Information is typed on word-processing systems in the department where it originates and a computer diskette is sent to the BI department, which then enters the information into the system, while monitoring it at the same time (see Figure 5–8). Then the information is available on-line to all users. More will be said about computers in the chapter on storage and dissemination.

Such sophisticated technology as the last two items may be out of reach for many companies, and it is enough to use simpler methods that are reinforced with vigorous management support to ensure effective communication. You should not lose sight of the fact that the purpose is, after all, to move data, and different methods will be appropriate to each organization and its employees. The general principles behind any good network communication, however, remain constant: It's essential (1) to establish formal communication channels and acceptable alternatives, and (2) to review these communication channels with the ICN, and inform the entire organization about them through the intelligence awareness briefing (see below).

Even with the establishment of a formal collection network and an "official" communication method, a considerable amount of data will be circulated directly by managers to their own network. This is unavoidable and not completely undesirable. One consumer electronics company had been subscribing to close to 100 trade, general business, and technical magazines. These magazines, each with a routing list of approximately eight names, were circulated among staff and line managers. As is the case in most companies, seldom did managers have the time to read the magazines: They would either accumulate in the to-be-read pile or continue circulation without being opened. An attempt to cut down on the number of magazines circulated to each manager met with vociferous resistance, despite the promise that librarians would scan the magazines and route relevant articles to managers. Managers claimed that they had to see the whole magazine because often they did not know in advance

Figure 5–8. Intelligence distribution and the computer.

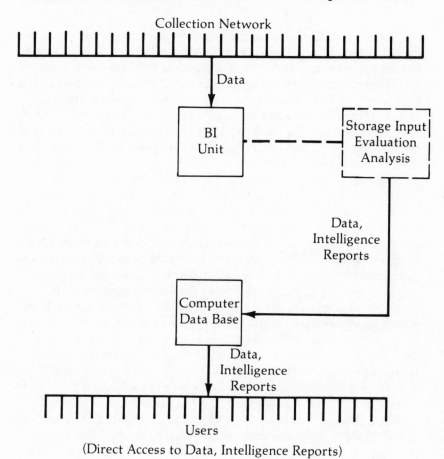

what would be of interest or relevance. Articles occasionally generated new ideas, thoughts, and avenues to explore, and these were novel slants that they could not think of ahead of time. Several also mentioned that they scanned competitors' ads in those magazines. Thus, while the formal business intelligence communication would cut down the amount of data that is circulated, it would not, and should not, completely eliminate the informal framework.

Educating and Motivating Collectors

After the methods of communicating data are firmly established, the next step should be to educate collectors and potential collectors as to their expected role and their specific tasks within the framework of the BI effort. Interviews with potential collectors at several companies who were in the process of establishing a formal business intelligence system revealed that many managers and employees were enthusiastic about the BI effort and would readily participate in it. Most of them, however, were at a loss as to what was actually required of them. For this reason, a program of educating the ICN should be an integral part of the implementation of a BI program.

It is also possible that for many targets no one in the organization will have already established information sources. Thus, if the intelligence is not currently accessible to members of the organization, the task of building the ICN becomes the task of identifying those people in the organization who will be capable and willing to access the pertinent sources. This is called planned coverage. In general, and whenever practical, it is better to devote one meeting to discussing how to approach the task of collection than just to tell the collectors to pick up data on certain targets as they read the technical journals, or to ask them to question their outside contacts about company X. In a sense, a coverage plan is the BI system's equivalent to management by objectives (MBO): Goals, targets, and their CINs are set, and sources are chartered—to the extent that the collector is willing to discuss them—so that the collection effort can be directed.

The issue of education goes hand in hand with that of motivation. Since the operation and productivity of the BI system depend on the good will, initiative, and participation of the total organization, motivation is the number one issue faced by the executive or individual who sets out to institute a full-scale BI program that would last beyond the span of a few months.

A variety of motivational techniques can be used, ranging from monetary incentives to promotions, but the best way to motivate is to instill in employees the sense of the importance of the undertaking to the success of the organization in the marketplace. That does not mean that material incentives are unimportant. One company, for example, announced to its sales force that 30 percent of the commission paid to salespeople would be devoted to rewards for intelligence about a particular product of the competition. Particularly, the management wanted information about the special niches and uses for the competitor's product. The operation was in effect for nine months, and, despite the initial negative response of salespeople, once they fully participated, the results were even more dramatic than expected. In fact, the salespeople benefited because the project gave them insights into new markets and new ways in which they could sell their own product.

Of course, not every company is willing or capable of diverting 30 percent of commissions to rewarding intelligence collection. There are other incentives close in nature to monetary incentives that seem to be effective in motivating collectors. One such incentive is to give weight to intelligence activities in promoting employees. In such cases, the manager recommending the employee for promotion consults the business intelligence unit or the department BI coordinator as a basis for such recommendations. This process therefore requires that the track record of collectors be maintained for ongoing reference.

Quite often motivating collectors is accomplished by "soft" organizational techniques, such as the consistent use of feedback. Employees are not averse to devoting extra time and effort to improve the company's BI capabilities, and often the knowledge that one contributed actively to the success of an overall strategy is a source of pride. Companies that have succeeded in maintaining this sense of pride, participation in, and creation of value for the organization use a combination of the following techniques:

- Top management showed continuous interest and support to the BI effort and its participants.
- BI personnel provided information of ongoing goals and BI needs.
- BI personnel provided regular feedback to collectors regarding the quality of their data and how useful the collected information was.

The support of top management is not to be overlooked. It is well known in management theory that if top management instills its values throughout the corporation, employees will follow. We were once told by a top executive of a large corporation that among its 12 subsidiaries, the most successful ones were, without exception, those where management was intelligence oriented. Top management creates the intelligence-oriented environment and culture, and culture is the utmost motivator. We have seen a BI system falling apart, despite a very professional BIU staff, because the firm where it was operating was acquired by another firm whose management was not interested in the intelligence gathering of the BIU. Thus, despite the fact that intelligence system activities were not actually discouraged, the lack of active support reduced the BI activities to marginal. A related problem is that in many companies the interest of top management in the subject is characterized by spurts of zeal followed by periods of complete neglect. Such practices are a source of frustration to those who champion BI within corporations, and ultimately the BI effort may fail unless the executive in charge is extremely tenacious.

On the other hand, the active encouragement by top management, who consistently and adequately reward those who help to provide the vital intelligence, can promote a business intelligence system to which many employees contribute. At one company, every quarter the most active and successful BI collectors were chosen to attend a briefing by top management. At the meeting management briefed employees about the company's competitive environment and the company's strategies. It was considered a great honor to be selected to attend these meetings. Employees felt that they were brought into the inner circle of those determining the company's future. The feeling of being at the center of decision making, of being part of those who were in the know, was a tremendous motivator. At another company, a weekly list was compiled of contributions by collectors and was sent to top management. The knowledge that such a list existed was in itself a sufficient motivator.

The role of the BI personnel in motivating the ICN is more specific. The BI personnel should keep the network "wet." Wetting the ICN means keeping it constantly updated on changing needs and targets—there is nothing more discouraging than collecting information that no one wants anymore—and telling the collectors when their data proved to be valid and important and when not. The first task may be achieved by circulating an internal newsletter devoted to intelligence. A newsletter serves both informational and motivational purposes. Also, by distributing it widely, one raises the awareness of all employees to the need for intelligence. Since a newsletter is distributed widely and therefore has the likelihood of also falling into the hands of competitors, caution must be taken that it does not contain information that could be damaging to the company.

The task of providing feedback about the quality and significance of the data is an important function of the BI personnel. The task is relatively easy if the company maintains a computerized data base of intelligence data, including, of course, field data. If pieces of data are referenced by their collector, it is possible to sort and retrieve data and provide collectors, or departments, specific input about the usefulness of the material they collected. Such feedback can prove very effective especially at the initial setting-up stage, since it guides BI collectors as to what information is useful and should be collected.

The intelligence awareness briefing serves a forum for providing feedback, as well as conveying other information indispensible for the establishment and ongoing management of the BI system. The goals of the briefing are (1) to communicate to as many employees as possible the existence of the BI program; (2) to motivate employees to join the ICN; (3) to educate employees in the procedures of the program, whether they will use them in the present or some future time; and (4) to provide a forum for discussion about how the BI system should operate, and air problems employees may have with collection of data.

The briefings should be conducted separately in each department or functional area so that the audience remains small and specific issues relating to that area are discussed. But the intelligence aware-ness briefing does not have to be limited to one forum or another. At one company a briefing was given as part of the annual sales meeting. In that manner management hoped to establish BI collection as part of the salespersons' responsibilities.

An intelligence awareness briefing lasts between two hours and half a day, depending on the extent of the training involved. A briefing can be an informal affair or a formal workshop, as outlined in the suggested agenda for an intelligence awareness briefing in Figure 5–9. This program is a half-day program.

The discussion of the importance of the BI effort should explain the goal of the BI system. In order to overcome employees' natural aversion to "spying," the subject of BI should be explicitly distin-guished from industrial espionage. The role of BI as a competitive tool in the fight for survival should be stressed. It is our experience that in corporations where the link of BI to the success of the business, and therefore to job security and prosperity, was explained convincingly, the motivation to help the corporation increased spec-tacularly. We have also found that examples of successful BI, as well as famous BI failures, help to convey the message effectively.

One incident we have recounted in many briefing sessions is about a company that manufactured a product used by the automo-

Figure 5–9.   The intelligence awareness briefing.

General Background
   Explain why division, or company, is embarking on the
      BI effort
   Explain the importance of business intelligence

What to Look For
   Provide a list of targets and priorities
   Provide examples of things the department should look
      for and items of particular interest to BIU

Where to Find Information
   Brief collectors on potential sources of information and
      solicit them for ideas

Techniques of Field Intelligence Collection
   Discuss legal and ethical issues in collection
   Outline basics of intelligence collection and field
      interviews
   Discuss issues of counterintelligence and security

Reporting Field Intelligence
   Discuss how, to whom, and when to communicate
      intelligence through formal channels
   Discuss how to establish the reliability of a source

Incentives
   Discuss any incentive system that will be implemented
   Discuss feedback that will be provided

---

bile industry. For years, the company was number two in the market, where market share was based essentially on quality. Then sales started to slip, and continued to decline despite promotional efforts by the company. When the situation deteriorated further, the company hired a consultant, who did a thorough BI job. First, the consultant talked to the number one and number three firms in the industry; they assured him that the claim of his client to the number two spot was well justified. Then he purchased five of the best-selling products on the market. He sent them to a lab that returned the surprising report showing that three of the products had a higher quality than his client's. Added to the surprise was the fact that two of the three products were from South America, not well known for producing this particular product. Investigating further, the consultant found out that the two products were actually manufactured in Japan, and distributed through a South American outlet to avoid alarming the American competitors. Indeed, none of the three leading firms suspected anything. The story does not have a happy ending: The company never regained its market share and was eventually sold by the parent company. If the company had had a system for tracking the competitive environment, management might have become aware much earlier, at least before sales deteriorated substantially, of the existence of foreign-manufactured competing products that were taking away market share.

The intelligence awareness briefing should serve as a forum for explaining the BI targets and intelligence information that the BI department is seeking. The possible sources of the information to which the group might have access should also be discussed. There is no need to reveal the entire list of targets and CINs, which can only confuse employees. Nevertheless, if collection is to be useful, the employees need to know what is relevant and what information is not relevant.

It is also important to inform employees on the procedures to report intelligence data. Even if the briefing does not yield immediate results, in the form of volunteer collectors, knowing where to bring data will pay off in the long run.

Each briefing should also be used to drill into employees the importance of elementary counterintelligence measures. The essence of a good intelligence strategy is that it extracts as much as possible from and about others, while simultaneously divulging as little as possible about the company and safeguarding its information. This principle becomes especially relevant when it comes to employees with extensive dealings with competitors' personnel, such as scientists who attend conferences, and executives. An effective BI network within a "leaky" organization is somewhat self-defeating.

The awareness briefing can serve to tighten control over the practices of BI already in use in the organization by bringing into the open the issues of ethics and legality in business intelligence. In addition to stating very clearly what is illegal—perhaps by using a representative from the legal department—the issue of what is moral is extremely important. Companies who have started a formal business intelligence program have established, as part of the program, guidelines as to what behavior is considered acceptable and unacceptable. For example, a company may prohibit misrepresentation when seeking information and may require the employee to identify himself fully. Therefore, an employee cannot collect information under the guise of a journalist writing an article, or obtain information from a competitor over the phone by claiming to be an engineering student writing a term paper.

The awareness briefing should be restricted as much as possible to homogeneous groups, such as sales personnel or R&D people. This permits the content of the briefing to be tailored to the needs and capabilities of the particular group. Another reason is that different departments have access to different sources and therefore will obtain different kinds of information. Similarly, the amount of information about the system divulged during the briefing to the various groups will be different. The salespeople do not need to know about the interest of management in particular technologies—a simple counterintelligence measure—while the briefing to the R&D group will naturally concentrate on these targets and CINs.

To sum up the points about the intelligence awareness briefing, we suggest you do the following test to see if your company needs the briefing. Ask yourself the following question: If an employee in your company accidentally heard about a competitor's plan to start a market test in the very near future of a revolutionary product that can reduce your market share to zero, does your worker know where and to whom to convey this information? Would he or she even know that this is a relevant piece of intelligence? Would he or she care enough to report it?

Keep in mind that the briefing is more than a method of disseminating information about the BI program and recruiting potential collectors. It is equivalent to the famous internal meetings of IBM salespeople in which the company's philosophy is conveyed to the employees in what can be compared to a religious crusade. Although every BI officer will not be an evangelist, creating a network of loyal employees akin to the BI culture of the Japanese corporation, can only be done by bringing employees to understand the value of their contribution to the survival of the corporation—and therefore their own jobs—in the face of growing competition. Such understanding can come about through a series of well-prepared and executed awareness briefings. It is our experience that when the CEO is intelligence-minded and works hard to instill this attitude in all employees, the amount of intelligence increases severalfold.

Managing the Collection Network

Once the network is in place, the work is not done. A collection network that is left alone after an initial push will come to a halt unless it is managed effectively. The intelligence awareness briefing should become part of the ongoing process of the ICN and should be repeated periodically in every department. The collection committee should be formed, as described in the chapter on organizational structure. Its role is very important at the inception of the BI program, but no less important as the system continues to expand and evolve.

When establishing the system, one should also keep in mind that it does not become fully operational immediately. On the contrary, the building up of the system is a slow, time-consuming process and may take months to show real results. However, it is a good idea to establish its usefulness and effectiveness early on, if only to demonstrate to management that it is worth the effort.

A company that regularly participated in government bids was submitting a proposal for a particularly large and important government project. Obtaining the project was very important to the company's survival. Yet, the consensus in the industry was that another company was emerging as a very strong competitor. Management wanted to estimate how low they had to bid to outbid the competitor. For that purpose they needed to know more about the competitor's latest investment in sophisticated computerized manufacturing equipment. It so happened that at the time an intelligence audit had been conducted at the company, followed by initial meetings to establish a collection network. At the briefing it was learned that the manager in charge of capital equipment purchasing, as well as the production manager, had a lot of information about the latest capital equipment purchases by the competitor. The information was quickly used in estimating new production costs for the competitor and helped in establishing a competitive bidding price for the project. Needless to say, this information established early on the value of the collection network and contributed to management's enthusiasm for the BI program.

The ultimate form that the collection network will take may be different than the way it operates initially. For example, a data collection system such as the written intelligence report (WIR) system works smoothly in a mature business intelligence system. In a young and growing system other methods of collection may have to supplement the official reporting system until the process is streamlined. There are several reasons for this:

1. Those in charge of managing the collection process have only limited knowledge of what information is available to the collectors. Through an intelligence audit it is possible to gain only partial knowledge of the wealth of field information that may be accessible by collectors. The full picture will be revealed only through experience in running the system for a few months and conducting repeated briefings and meetings of the collection committee.

2. Even when given a list of targets, new collectors may not be able to relate the list to the information they know.

3. The initiation of the intelligence reporting system where it has not been used before will provide only current information. It may be possible to tap into past knowledge of particular individuals by using other means of collection.

For these reasons, when initiating a communications system, collectors and BI personnel need to work together much more closely. Through the initial stages of implementing the collection network, some of the collection effort should be carried out by conducting interviews with groups of collectors within each functional area. These collection interviews will offer immediate feedback to both collectors and the BIU that directs the collection process, and will speed up the educational process for both sides.

When the ICN is established and the BI specialists begin to request information from the field, it is not wise to overly restrict the kind of information requested from particular collectors. This means that the list of targets and priorities should be broad enough, and although some guidelines for collection by each department should be provided, collectors should be encouraged at first to collect and transmit a broad spectrum of data, which may or may not seem to be important. When these bits and pieces of both published and field data are accumulated over time, a clear idea will emerge of which bits and pieces are useful in putting together a picture of the competition. Furthermore, based on the knowledge gained over the initiation phase of the collection network, changes can be made in the list of items that should be collected and communicated by the collection network.

Such a process of slowly introducing an ICN to the organization of a defense contractor proved very effective. In this particular situation the quality assurance department had been collecting information about the quality assurance programs of competitors. This information helped them conceive better quality assurance programs for the company itself. With the new collection network in place, QA began to forward all that detailed information to the BIU. Most of these details about the competitors' quality assurance programs proved useless in determining important factors regarding competitors, such as their cost structure, so it was decided that this information was only useful to the QA department and should not be transmitted to the BIU; instead summaries of important competitive data about quality would be routed to the staff preparing the five-year plan. These executives and analysts needed that type of information without realizing it was collected by the QA department. Moreover, when initially encouraging collection and transmission of a wide range of data, the BI people found out that the engineers' trip reports contained information which was valuable to the strategic planning department, although it was obscured by tons of technical jargon.

Final Word

The work of the ICN can be augmented through buying the services of outside collectors, such as intelligence research firms, market research firms, and consultants. Both internal and external collection are useful, each within its own limitations. Intelligence generated by the ICN is not always sufficient, especially when the intelligence needed relates to new markets or industries in which the company is not currently involved. In this case it is unlikely that the BI system will be able to generate enough in-depth information. Also, some outside services, such as clipping services and companies providing Freedom of Information Act documents, are essential tools for the BI unit. Another reason that companies use outside research services is to keep the name of the company confidential. Thus, outside collectors supplement the ICN. Unfortunately, the rush of many companies to hire expensive intelligence collection services is an example of wasted resources. Instead, we suggest the use of internal resources whenever they are effective.

6

BI Sources—An Overview

Sources for business information are most commonly identified with published sources of information: newspapers, business magazines, trade journals, Wall Street reports. There are thousands of such sources, and several excellent guides to them. In this chapter we do not intend to compete with these reference books. Instead, we give a quick overview of the categories of important sources, and refer the reader to detailed guides for further information. We offer a word of warning, though. There is a tendency among some consultants in the new field of BI to give the impression that a list of hundreds of sources is a necessary and sufficient basis for good BI. We believe that an intelligence *system* is the managerial tool that is the answer to the growing need for good intelligence in decision making, not a reference book of endless sources. BI has much more to it than understanding *where* to find information. It is *how* to organize the search and *what* to do with the findings that really matters.

In addition to published sources, there are field, or human, sources. Field sources are extremely important to an effective BI system. This chapter includes a list of generic categories of field sources. You and others in your organization may be able to identify additional field sources, unique to your company, market, or industry. We also present a table comparing field and published sources. Our conclusion is not that published sources are useless, but that they must be supplemented with information from field sources to provide both background and critical intelligence.

Published Sources

Published sources can be categorized into three broad classes: what others say about the competitors, what the competitors say about themselves, and the government as a source of intelligence.

What Others Say About the Competitors

Books. They're a relatively inexpensive source that can provide some insight into the way your competitor thinks. A case in point is the book by DeLorean about GM.

Business reference books. A starting place for any research is the reference material. The list includes directories of companies (such as *Dun's Million Dollar Directory*), bibliographies (and other business information sources), indexes to periodicals and newspapers (the *Business Periodical Index*, for instance), corporate background information (*Standard and Poor's Corporation Records*), industry statistical compilations (*Predicasts*), financial information about companies provided by investment services (*Moody's Manuals*), and directories to associations (such as the *American Bank Directory*). Although the material in directories may not be completely up-to-date, it provides background information, and names of industry experts.

Business periodicals. Business magazines provide recent gossip and intelligence, as well as analysis. Some of them, such as *Fortune* and *Inc.*, offer unique compilations of corporate data. They are also a prime source for broad-issue scanning.

Trade press. Trade literature is probably the number one published source read and used by executives. It includes such information as personnel changes, background on people in the industry, meetings, new products, and appointments of agents.

Local press. Local newspapers and magazines provide surprises to the reader who can wade through all the wedding announcements. Information on plant locations, expansion plans, internal promotions, lawsuits, employee programs, environmental concerns, and so on are to be found in the regional sources. Several information service companies offer the service of tracking local newspapers.

Industry and company research. This is usually quite expensive, unless you are able to obtain reports through personal relationships, such as directly from Wall Street analysts. These sources provide statistics and industry and company information compiled by securities analysts, government analysts, and consulting firms.

Technical journals. They monitor trends in technology. Your R&D people are probably subscribing to many of the technical journals for their own purposes. Asking them to mark relevant passages is a quick way to access this source. The same is true for academic publications in areas such as management, marketing, and finance.

What Competitors Say About Themselves

Books and articles. Top executives who write about themselves and their companies provide a limited view into the workings of these corporations. Examples are Lee Iacocca's recent biography and Greenwood's account of planning at GE. Similarly, articles in professional publications by executives may reveal some inside information, especially if they use actual anecdotes to support their arguments. An example of such a publication is the *Planning Review,* a professional journal for planners.

Speeches and announcements. These reveal management philosophies and intentions. *The Wall Street Transcript* contains a compilation of speeches by company officials to securities analysts.

Advertising. It provides information on how the competitor positions its product line and the markets it targets. Want ads, on the other hand, may point to future strengths, especially in technical areas, and to stability of management.

Internal literature. This is often a very good published source about a company's strategy, management philosophy, and future plans. Internal newsletters are not always easy to obtain, but since they have wide distribution among employees, customers, and retired employees, they are not out of reach. Internal publications also include executives' speeches, promotional announcements, announcements of incentive programs, and the like. Since the purpose of these publications is to communicate information to employees, it is difficult for the editors to prevent intelligence from leaking to outsiders. Most corporations, though aware of the problem, still believe that the benefit to the morale of the employees outweighs the cost in breaches of security. This fact makes the publications valuable to you.

Annual reports. The reports reveal priorities, investment strategy, plans for growth, goals, even inconsistencies in policies. Footnotes to the financial statements reveal problems to those who know how to read them. The need to appear optimistic in public makes some of the reports less useful, but tracking and comparing reports of several years may reveal trends in management thinking.

Testimony, lawsuits, antitrust information. Court records that can be inspected include transcripts, evidence, testimony, and judgments in civil and criminal cases. These data can be quite interesting, considering the cases of bankruptcies, customer complaints, and disputes with creditors that can be investigated. Alas, the complexity of the court system and the regulations governing the release of information are a nightmare to nonlawyers.

Government as a Source of Intelligence

Government is a big collector of information. The problem with this source of information is that it is typically outdated, and companies filing with the government are bound to reveal as little as legally possible. Still, for background material as well as some exotic data found nowhere else, this is the place to look.

Getting the information from the federal government is facilitated (some would say hindered) by the Freedom of Information Act, enacted in 1966. The act mandates the release of any identifiable records of the administrative agencies in the executive branch of the federal government, unless the document falls into one of nine exemption categories. The last restriction limits the usefulness of government as an intelligence source, but does not eliminate it completely. Since final decisions regarding the release of information are left with the officers of the agency, you may get information your competitors would rather have remain confidential.

If you find the bureaucratic maze too taxing, we recommend two methods that make it easier and more efficient to use government documents as a source. The first is to ask the legal department and controller's office at your company for a list and samples of the type of filing your company is required to do with the government (federal, state, and local). Once you are familiar with the type of information your company is required to divulge, you are familiar also with the type of information your competitors are required to submit. Second, use one of the information services that specialize in tracking and extracting information from the government—for example, FOI Services, Inc., especially for information filed with the FDA and EPA, and Disclosure, Inc., for documents filed with the SEC. Consult one of the many business research reference books for a list of information service companies.

Among the various federal agencies, there are some that are more valuable sources of information for business researchers. The following is a list of these with a short description of the type of information they collect.

Securities and Exchange Commission. The SEC collects financial and a host of other information on all public companies in the United States, as well as on investment management companies and stockbrokers. Among the more exotic forms filed with the SEC are documents by foreign firms selling stock in the U.S., details on tender offers, and background and future plans of a person or company that has acquired more than five percent of the securities of a publicly traded company.

Food and Drug Administration. The FDA collects information on food, drug, cosmetic, and other related manufacturers, from plant inspection reports and background information for drug approval to research projects.

Internal Revenue Service. Some financial information on nonprofit organizations is available to the public.

U.S. Patent Office. The only problem is that some companies file patents on unsuccessful products to mislead the competition. Here, nothing will help but good field intelligence.

Federal Trade Commission. Documentation of FTC investigations into antitrust matters are released to the public.

U.S. Consumer Product Safety Commission. It releases reports on investigations of companies and products, and also reports listing complaints and corrective actions.

Environmental Protection Agency. Information is furnished on chemical companies, including plant size and production volume.

Department of Labor. Information is related to the department's jurisdiction over working conditions, labor training, collective bargaining, workers' compensation, and more.

U.S. Geological Survey. Aerial maps, an exotic but sometimes useful source for information on facilities used by competitors, can reveal plant additions and reductions. They are available from both the federal and state (especially highway) authorities; the U.S. Geological Survey provides a master index to them.

U.S. government research and development reports. This source covers scientific and technical information from contracts awarded by the government for R&D, and is useful for companies dealing with the government, such as defense contractors, although it also provides a glimpse of technology for related fields.

Congressional committee hearings. These include pending regulations, and investigations of products, companies, and business practices. There are indexes and information services to help you find your way through the endless number of House and Senate committees.

Some of the more exotic documents are available from offices such as the World Traders Data Reports Section at the Department of Commerce (information on foreign companies dealing with U.S. firms); the Office of Pension Programs at the Labor Department (information on corporate pension agreements); the U.S. Customs Service (information on the effect of imports); and the National Labor

Relations Board (information on investigations of unfair labor practices).

In addition, several government agencies publish aggregate statistical data about industries, which are available to the public. Among the more notable are the Department of Commerce publications, from census reports to economic analyses, and the Department of Labor publications such as the Bureau of Labor Statistics compilation on employment, prices, and productivity. The IRS also publishes a sourcebook of statistics of income based on company tax returns. All that information is historical and aggregate, but can serve as background to proposals and strategic analyses.

In addition to the federal government, you can turn to the state and local authorities. State agencies collect financial and organizational information, conduct investigations of businesses and plants, inspect the workplace for safety violations, collect background information for licensing purposes, require franchisers to file records with the state, and much more. In addition, state offices publish annual statistics on industries in the state. Most of the records of state agencies are available under state laws.

Local authorities are full of surprising records. Local courthouse files on competitors' building permits and plans are available. Details on real estate transactions, size and volume of plants, and consumer complaints against smaller firms situated in the locality are examples of other data accessible to the public and the inquiring mind of the intelligence officer.[1]

Using Data Bases

A special category of published sources are computerized data bases. There are more than 2000 on-line data bases available today, both bibliographical, which provide references only, and full-text data bases. There are several points to remember when approaching the issue of data bases. If you decide to subscribe to one or several data base publishers and conduct your own search, as more and more companies are opting to do, you will need to train your

---

[1]For an extensive list of sources we recommend *Competitor Intelligence*, a source reference book by Leonard Fuld (1985), and the various guides to sources published by Washington Researchers, a research firm based in Washington, D.C.

employees in methods of effective search. For example, if you need a small number of highly relevant references and the search concepts are simple, you can use an index term. If you want to canvass a topic comprehensively, the search concepts are new or complex, and abstracts are representative of the document content, you may use a free-text search. The alternative is to hire the services of a company specializing in searching data bases. It is desirable to keep in mind, though, that the information available on data bases is often not up to date and it may be hard to find the particular piece that is relevant. Therefore, you should consider carefully the expenditure on data bases and data base searches.

Field Sources

A truly effective BI system combines the information obtained from research of published data with the more current, if slightly less reliable, field intelligence. If the former is a necessary input, the latter is a critical one for decision making. We classify field sources in two ways: what others say about the competitors, and what competitors say about themselves.

What Others Say About the Competitors

Customers. Customers can provide information about competitor products, plans to introduce a new product, pricing, service, personnel and personnel changes, planned plant locations, and strategic changes, among other things. According to several studies of scanning behavior of managers in the U.S. and abroad, customers are the primary source for market and competitive intelligence. In tapping this source, you should note that purchasing agents of the customers have a lower reliability as a source than the customers' top management and engineers. One company taught their salespeople to perform elementary service on their product, office automation equipment, to get beyond the customers' purchasing departments for the sole purpose of gathering intelligence.

Suppliers. Second only to customers as sources of competitive and market intelligence, suppliers can provide a wide range of data about competitors. You should recognize that suppliers comprise more than just sellers of materials to the company. Banks, advertising agencies, and public relations firms all have an incentive to provide data to you. Moreover, biases in the data are relatively easy to recognize. Suppliers, because they are motivated by the desire to sell their products, will provide detailed information about previous transactions, some of them with competitors. For example, a supplier of computerized manufacturing systems provided detailed information about the recent purchase of capital equipment by a competitor, including the exact specifications of the equipment and the purpose of the purchase.

Dealers, agents, and distributors. Retailers or wholesalers are known to have very useful gossip about competitors, foreign competition, changes in product lines, pricing, and promotion.

Consultants. Though operating under confidentiality agreements, and less updated than the other sources mentioned previously, consultants accumulate broad knowledge of industry trends and practices that can be used for strategic intelligence.

Job candidates. See entry on p. 99.

Unions. A very good source on labor unrest, wage rates, impending strikes, employment conditions, and details regarding specific labor contracts with particular companies.

Trade associations. The main usefulness of contacts at the trade association is in providing general industry data. The officers of the association know that in order to keep the lines of communication open they should have the confidence of their members. Therefore they usually give out only general industry information.

Chambers of commerce. Especially in locations where your competitor has its plants, the local chamber of commerce can provide employment data, data about size of the competitor's facility, interest of companies in relocating, consumer complaints against local businesses, and more.

Local development corporations. Often they can provide information regarding a new plant opened by the competitor, if the agency had been involved in the financing of the project. Information they have is about the terms of the financing, the size of the facility, any tax incentives for the company, information about employees hired and to be hired, training that the company provides, expected total payroll, and wage rates.

Subcontractors. As suppliers of your company, subcontractors are bound to do similar jobs for your competitors. It can't hurt to try and extract intelligence from them.

Security analysts. Wall Street analysts have intimate knowledge about industries and companies. Although they are bound by confidentiality as far as information that they have not made public, they may be willing to discuss unpublished information that is not confidential.

Journalists. They're excellent sources, particularly those who work in local press and trade journals. Journalists usually put into their articles only a fraction of the background research and detail about an article topic. They can therefore be a good source of additional information beyond what appeared in a particular article. Although often busy and hard to get, they are open to sharing information, especially if you reciprocate. They are also good sources for leads and additional contacts.

Watchdog groups. Consumer unions, the Better Business Bureau, and environmentalist groups are but a few.

Regulators and government analysts. Everyone knows the story that somewhere in Washington there is a government analyst who is dying to tell you everything you want to know. Some of those analysts have been at their jobs for many years and are waiting patiently for you to call and pick their brains. The problem is finding those analysts in the bureaucratic maze.

Field sources are only limited by your imagination. The places where you will find information are sometimes surprising and unexpected. For example, one BI specialist discovered that some of the résumés of job applicants received by the human resources department had organization charts attached showing the applicant's position in his or her current employer's organization. Using this information, details of several competitors' organizations were pieced together.

What Competitors Say About Themselves

Plant tours. They're not as popular today as they were a few years ago, before American companies realized that all those Japanese tourists taking pictures were actually gathering intelligence. Your purchasing department employees may have knowledge of and access to plant tours of your competitors.

Annual meetings. Sometimes they are fun, especially if disgruntled groups attempt a proxy fight. Other times, they may provide a glimpse at management style. All you need is to own a few shares of the competition. If you attempt to buy more than five percent, though, the SEC will want to know your intentions and may not believe your story about intelligence gathering at annual meetings.

Court appearances. Antitrust cases and litigation against former employees might be interesting. Your legal department can alert you or serve as a collector for this source.

Technical conferences, trade shows, and conventions. These provide a natural place to gather intelligence. Note, though, that the competition is there to do the same. It boils down to who is a smarter intelligence collector. IBM, for example, briefs participants at technical meetings to keep their mouths shut. Other companies may be less security-conscious. Much industry gossip is passed along during trade meetings, and the competitors' new products and product literature are available for inspection. Also, the competitors' representatives are there to answer questions. Technical conferences are worthwhile because you can get a glimpse into the research conducted by competitors and learn about the backgrounds of their engineers and scientists.

Speeches. Officers make speeches to Wall Street analysts, local high schools, and chambers of commerce. Attending these meetings and asking a few questions is the bread and butter of some of the executives in your company. Direct them and use them as collectors.

Information from job candidates.   Candidates interviewed for job openings at your company are potential sources of information. However, most managers consider it unethical to place a want ad solely for the purpose of interviewing employees of competitors in order to gain information. What is acceptable, to most managers, is to make use of intelligence data gained from job candidates answering bona fide employment ads. In such interviews the questions to the candidate are not posed with intelligence collection in mind, and any information provided voluntarily by the candidate is a by-product of the interview. It is nevertheless advisable for the interviewer or the BI staff using the candidate's data to make sure that the information provided is not proprietary to the candidate's current employer.

Information from new employees.   If asking job applicants to provide intelligence data about their employers is unethical, asking new employees with relevant background to help the BI effort of the company is more acceptable. Again the new employee should never be pressed into providing the data about the former employer. In any case, only information that is not considered proprietary should be asked for. Some employees may have signed confidentiality agreements with their former employer and are even more restricted in what they will say.

To effectively make use of the valuable data available from new employees, we suggest that the human resources department of your company report regularly to the BI unit about new professional employees and managers hired and forward their résumés for review. The BI staff could then determine if the background of the new employee is relevant to the company BI targets. If it is, the BI unit should hold a debriefing session. To prevent resentment we recommend that the debriefing be conducted by the head of the department of the new employee and with the representative of the BI unit present. The interview should be conducted only with the consent of the new employee and no undue pressure should be put on the employee to talk about topics with which he or she is uncomfortable. The employee should be assured of the right not to answer any question. The briefing itself should be friendly. The questions should not deal with trade secrets or other data that should not be revealed by the employee. On the other hand, new employees are excellent sources of data about management personality and style, organizational dynamics, and organizational strategies.

Table 6–1. Comparison of published sources and field sources.

	Published	Field
Timeliness	Never too recent	Usually immediate
Level of aggregation	Relatively high	Discrete and specific
Depth	Broad coverage; in-depth analysis	Narrower coverage; specific pieces of data
Cost	Some public sources very expensive, others free	No cost, except collectors' time
Reliability and validity	Prestigious sources maintain high reliability and validity	Difficult to determine
Relevance	To a large extent externally determined	Can be directed

Final Word

The best BI system uses both published and field sources. In reality, published sources are used by strategic planning units, environmental scanning units, corporate economists, and researchers. Field sources are used more by line management. This dichotomy is the inevitable result of the access that the two groups have to different sources of information. The essence of our *system* approach to BI, with the emphasis on the internal network of collectors, is to bring together the information from the two types of sources. Thus, we stress the deployment of salespeople and R&D personnel as part of the same BI program, reporting to the same agency—be it a BI unit, or a part-time BI specialist—that will ensure that material as diverse as that gleaned from technical journals and rumored from customers are pieced together to suggest a rounded picture of the competition. It is useful for the person who combines the data from the two types of sources to keep in mind the difference between them. For that purpose we present a brief comparison between the two in Table 6–1.

7

Evaluation

Now that the ICN is in place and begins to report data to the person in charge of receiving it, the second stage of the intelligence system takes place: evaluation.

Evaluation of data is the first *processing* step. It precedes analysis, as the following list indicates.

How Raw Data Are Processed

To create useful intelligence, each piece of raw data is

1. obtained
2. abstracted or "translated"
3. stored or categorized
4. collated

5. evaluated
6. analyzed
7. plugged into the puzzle
8. projected

The above list describes the journey a piece of data takes from its raw datum form to its place as part of the final intelligence picture, which serves as the backbone of decision making. The purpose of analysis is to produce intelligence. Intelligence is the systematically organized and integrated body of information digested and made relevant for decision making. Analysis therefore involves the organization of pertinent information, interpretation of the information, and extrapolation of the possible outcomes and their probability of occurrence. Analysis requires the understanding of competitive strategy, without which it is difficult to interpret events in the environment. Evaluation, on the other hand, is a more technical stage in the processing of data. Specifically, the purpose of evaluation is (1) to measure the usefulness of the data, and (2) to measure the usefulness of the source.

Data and source evaluation is the quality control function in the BI program. It is a collection of techniques used to assess the quality of the data collected, and to measure its reliability. In addition, evaluation helps to determine the adequacy of collection coverage of particular targets. Done properly, evaluation serves as an excellent filter, reducing the flood of data into a set of useful building blocks for analysis.

In intelligence services, military and governmental, evaluation is done formally, by specially trained staff, and is considered as important as the collection itself. In business intelligence programs, where resources are much scarcer, the evaluation process may not be carried out as rigorously. The BI specialist, however, should become familiar with the techniques and considerations of proper evaluation, so that whatever evaluation does take place, it is done effectively. One of the more famous examples of the role of evaluation is the success of the Allies' intelligence services—especially the British—during World War II in leading the Germans to believe that the invasion of Europe would not start at Normandy. The reason the Nazis believed the invasion would come from another direction was the ability of the British to establish *credibility* to the misinformation fed to the enemy. This is a rather dramatic example of the importance of evaluating data accurately. A BI specialist in a corporation may not deal with world-shaping events and information, but the evaluation of the reliability of an announcement about, for example, radical capacity expansion can determine the entire strategy of the corporation. This was the case, in fact, when Motorola and Texas Instruments fought an "announcement war" about capacity.

Evaluating Data: Data Usefulness

There are six components determining our judgment of the usefulness of data to the firm. To analyze data we should consider the following factors:

Relevance
Truth value

Understandability
Sufficiency
Significance
Timeliness

Not every bit of data that is true is relevant to the company, and not every relevant piece is significant. The usefulness of data is a complex concept, and though we do not always think of it consciously when we examine a report by a collector, the components above are what make (or should make) us decide that the particular datum is useful and should be further routed through the BI system.

Relevance

The issue of relevance of data is relatively straightforward. Here the analyst asks the questions: Are the data related to company goals or to company strategies? Are they about potential threats or opportunities? As straightforward as it may sound, it is far from a simple question to answer. One wonders, for example, if the IBM executive who first got wind of the two guys in California selling computer boards out of their basement answered "yes" to the question: Is this a potential threat or perhaps an opportunity? To judge by the length of time it took IBM to enter the market for personal computers, even in light of their familiar strategy of letting others create the market, it seems that someone at IBM was slow in realizing the relevance of the new technology.

Truth Value

The truth value of a piece of data seems to be the most elementary thing to consider in evaluating it. Yet it is also the most difficult to determine. To be accurate, there is no sure way to determine whether a piece of data is true or not, especially if the data is about an event that is to take place in the future. There are, however, indicators about the truth of data that should make one more confident about using them. The two indicators we use are reliability of the source and reliability of the data.

Reliability of the source. This is one indicator, though indirect, to the truth value of data. One question an analyst should ask is whether the source would benefit from accuracy of the data or from providing inaccurate data. An example is a job candidate who provides information about previous employers and would clearly benefit from accuracy. On the other hand, a source that provides seemingly excellent data without an apparent motive is to be suspected. Another question to ask is about the conditions under which the data were provided. The accuracy of a conversation over a third martini may be somewhat suspect (of course, there are always those who know someone who becomes coherent *only* after the third martini). Biasing conditions may include the physical setting, such as a bar; the mental or physical state of the source; and the motive (revenge is a biasing motive, friendship is an unbiasing one). Also, the method by which the source obtains the data suggests something about its truth. Firsthand data are generally better than hearsay. Data read in a serious publication as a rule are more reliable—though less significant and surely less timely—than field information. Finally, there is the question of how likely the data are to be known by the source. If a junior executive of a competitor divulges information that is typically known only to the top management of the organization, one should suspect the truth of the information.

Reliability of the data. The question of data reliability is whether the data can be verified independently of the source. The technique of verification is known as cross-validation and involves collecting data about the same subject from other sources, for the sake of comparison. Cross-validation can be done with established and unestablished facts. The first consists of already known facts about the target, such as a piece of data about a competitor being in financial trouble that can be compared and corroborated with previously discovered layoffs in some of its plants. A report about coming changes in top management can be corroborated with previously announced news about the resignation of certain executives.

Unestablished facts are other pieces of intelligence about the same subject that have not yet been verified. If several sources provide similar data about a particular R&D project, and these sources are relatively independent (that is, of various affiliations), then these reports are all unestablished "facts" but together, they corroborate each other. Similarly, if one source reports that a competitor is looking to change its ad agency, and another reports that the competitor is coming out with a new product, the two yet unestablished facts may to an extent cross-validate each other. Of course, there are many cases in which data are available from only one source, and no independent corroboration is possible. In these cases the truth value of the data may not be determinable beyond the application of commonsense judgment regarding the likelihood that the target will behave in the particular way suggested by the report, and the track record of the source of the information in past reporting. Such a record can be established only if someone tracks the reliability of the source over time, as forward-looking intelligence becomes present facts. This process is depicted in Figure 7–1.

At Time 1 (the present), the truth value of a piece of data is estimated, based on the reliability of both data and source. For example, a union contact tells one of your collectors that the leadership of the union has decided to strike your competitor around the end of the contract period, which is due at the end of the month. At the time the data are provided, no previous record is available on the source (the union man). Therefore, the only way to judge the truth of the data is to estimate its reliability by, say, calling on a contact within the competition and asking about the state of negotiations with the union, and other pertinent questions. This is a cross-validation method. In addition, perhaps someone at the purchasing

Figure 7–1.   The evaluation process: Estimating the truth value of data.

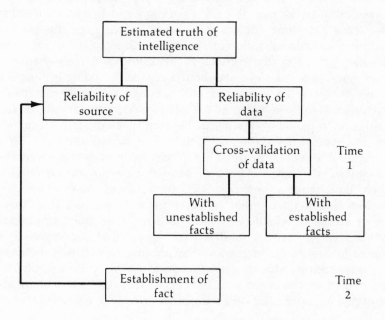

department sends an item stating that the competitor has reduced its purchase of raw materials in recent days. Then in Time 2 (say, the end of the month), if the competitor is indeed struck, the datum becomes a fact, and helps to establish the reliability of the source at the union. The established reliability will thereafter help to estimate the truth value of other data the source may eventually provide.

Understandability

Data may be provided by sources and collectors in many forms. Collectors in the sales force may report data in qualitative form and sales jargon. Your collectors in the financial department will report the same type of data in figures and in different terms. More important, the data may simply be unfamiliar to the analyst whose background is different from the collector's. In a typical BI unit, the analyst will be familiar with the industry and with the company's business in general, but data from the R&D department, legal collectors, and others could be too technical for the generalist to understand. In these cases, the analyst may decide that the data are useless, at least in their present form. Alternatively, the analyst might either ask the collector for clarification, or consult a company expert who is part of the technical advice network in the organization.

Sufficiency

Here the reader of the data asks the following questions: Can one draw meaningful conclusions from the data as is, regarding effects on the company? If the data are significant, are they sufficient to trigger action by someone in the company, or are additional data needed before a strategic or tactical move is made? Flexibility is a key characteristic of an effective BI system and if a piece of data is sufficiently significant and complete to draw conclusions that call for action, the analyst—or even the collector—should immediately communicate the message to the appropriate user. Also, sometimes a piece of data may look incomplete but is in effect the missing link essential to the understanding of other, already collected data. Therefore, it should receive a high mark on sufficiency. For example, one of your collectors reports that in a recent conversation she had with her friend from the chamber of commerce of her town, the friend discussed the number of employees in a competitor's plant at that town. This piece of data, combined with already collected data on hourly wages, pension benefits, and other labor compensation, can lead to the calculation of the cost of direct labor at the plant, and to an accurate assessment of the competitiveness of the other firm.

Significance

Significant data usually are those that warrant *immediate* action. If a piece of intelligence relates to an immediate opportunity or threat, the evaluator should realize that delay for further analysis may cause the firm irreversible damage. A report about a release date for a new product by a competitor is one example of data that should be immediately routed to the appropriate department for action, in this case to senior management and the marketing department for promotional campaign planning. It is very possible that the data will be reported by an employee that is not in the department, such as a PR employee who heard the news from a reporter friend. Certain data may not call for immediate action, but are significant in the overall effect they may have on strategic plans. A piece of data about social trends does not call for an immediate price/product mix change, but carries significant implications for the long-run strategy. An example is the implication to the tobacco industry of the change in the social acceptability of smoking.

Timeliness

The best piece of data is useless if it is already known to everyone in the industry. The timeliness of data involves their recency, the time lapse between collection and communication to the BI unit, and the extent of their exclusivity. A rule of thumb is that data appearing in publications are not timely: By the time they are published, everyone in the industry knows about them. Therefore, as a general rule, field data will be evaluated as more useful than published data.

Summary: Data Usefulness

The six factors the evaluator should weigh in judging the overall usefulness of the piece of data or a report are: relevance, truth value, understandability, sufficiency, significance, and timeliness. It should be emphasized that these factors serve as the basis for evaluation whether or not evaluation is done explicitly and formally, or implicitly and informally. In the latter case, the evaluator should simply keep in mind the various dimensions of usefulness in deciding what to do next with the data. Such rational but implicit evaluation usually becomes second nature to seasoned intelligence specialists. In a formal BI system, the evaluation may be done explicitly by the BI analyst. In both cases, the evaluator can use the first impression about the reliability of the source and the data as provided by the collector on the form used for BI reporting.

Such a procedure is especially useful when the report is expected to go for further processing to other people. For the people in the next, or higher, line of processing—for example, the director of the BI unit—the scoring system suggested below provides a quick and efficient way to evaluate the importance of the report at one glance.

There are several methods of assigning scores to the six factors. The simplest one is to assign a score to each factor using the letters H, M, and L, which stand for high, medium, and low. Another is to use numbers to create an ordinal scale with, say, 5 as the highest score and 1 as the lowest. It is worth noting that people using scales tend to give the middle score more often. Therefore, you might want to assign a neutral judgment of unknown reliability or average relevance to the mid scale. The evaluation of each of the six factors may trigger certain actions, and the overall usefulness of the data determines whether or not they will be stored permanently or used in analysis. Actions that follow particular evaluations were discussed earlier in relation to each factor. For example, a low score on understandability of data will require additional communication with the collector and/or internal consultants; a low score on sufficiency will trigger requests for additional collection; a high score on significance and timeliness will probably trigger immediate reporting to users; and so on. The overall judgment as to the value of the data follows two standard decision rules commonly used in decision theory: (1) the lexicographic filtering rule, and (2) the weighted value rule.

The lexicographic filtering rule is based on the importance of relevance and truth value in evaluation. For a piece of data to be considered further it must pass the test of these two factors with a minimum score (say, medium). If it fails, the piece can be discarded before any other factor is considered. The filter rule is a method by which the six factors are ranked according to their importance (for example, relevance is first, truth is second, significance is third, and so on) and each piece of data has to be filtered through each factor in order. If the item passes that factor with a minimum score, it is then considered against the next factor.

The second rule refers to the subjective weighting of factors by the evaluator. For example, one report (A) may be timely, understandable, and sufficient, but low on significance. It may need analysis, but not urgently. On the other hand, another report (B) may be insufficient and low on understandability, but the reader may suspect from the little that is understood that the subject matter of the report is very timely and significant. Report B will thus receive higher priority for analysis and storage than report A.

The two rules, filtering and weighted value, can be combined for a faster evaluation procedure. Thus, once a report is considered relevant and reasonably true—by virtue of the filtering method—the priority assigned to its further processing will be based on its overall weight, which in turn will be determined by the evaluator weighing the scores of the remaining four factors. We suggest in Table 7-1 the following scheme of priorities, but emphasize that it is the individual case that should prevail, not any rigid rule.

How to Detect Misinformation

While a piece of data goes through the evaluation process, it is desirable to keep in mind the possibility of misinformation or disinformation provided by the source or to the source for the purpose of misleading the collecting organization. The phenomenon of disinformation is not as rare as it may seem. Porter (1980, pp. 75–88)

Table 7-1. Priority of remaining usefulness factors.

Priority	High	Medium	Low
Understandability	M–H	L–M	L–H
Sufficiency	M–H	M–H	L–M
Significance	H	M–H	L–M
Timeliness	H	M–H	L–M

discusses the issue of "market signals" conveyed by one company to others, and disinformation is a legitimate, if dangerous, part of the psychological war of signaling intentions. There are several indications of disinformation:

1. If the information is "too good to be true," too complete, perfectly consistent, detailed, and extremely hard to get, one should suspect a setup.

2. If all sources report the same rumor at the same time, with little variation, suspect a deliberate leak. It is the nature of BI and people that no two sources tell exactly the same story.

3. If the source is unlikely to have had access to the type of data being supplied, it may be a case of boasting, or it may be that someone in the competitor organization is trying to uncover a leak. The trick of planting a false datum where only few know about it is an old method of discovering leaks. An example is a planted news item about an upcoming market test in a particular market. If the competitor reduces his prices in that location, a leak may have been discovered. Another example of planting misinformation to discover a leak is a false rumor about a top executive who seeks to move to the competition. If a contact is made with that executive, a leak can be discovered.

4. If the motivation of the source cannot be established, but the information is very useful and delicate, suspect a deliberate leak. Motives can range from friendship to revenge, but there is no free lunch. If information is provided for no apparent reason, it is better to treat it suspiciously than to act hastily.

Additional By-Products of Evaluation

The main purpose of the evaluation process is to decide which data become information for analysis and storage, and which can be discarded as irrelevant or unreliable. The BI evaluator, however, is in the unique position to use the process for other purposes as well, such as determining the adequacy of collection coverage.

The coverage of BI targets is a dynamic process. Targets change, collectors leave, sources dry out. All these changes necessitate the ongoing tracking of collection to see if it covers all targets properly. The activity of cross-evaluating reports, which is part of the overall evaluation process, enables the analyst to review the adequacy of coverage. If, over a period of time, only one source appears to provide data about a given target, that should trigger a search for additional coverage. Also, if data are scored low on sufficiency, and no additional data can be obtained when the analyst requests them, that should also signal inadequate coverage. Thus, while performing evaluations, the analyst is in a position to review the coverage of targets through the actual experience of trying to validate and complete the picture of the target.

Usefulness of Sources

The second major task of evaluation, besides the determination of the usefulness of the data, is to monitor the sources themselves. The determination of source usefulness serves two purposes: (1) It ensures optimal coverage of the established targets, and (2) it ensures the proper use of available resources. This second objective alone may sometimes justify putting a BI system in place. The money saved from discontinuing the purchase of expensive but less than useful published sources of data is surprisingly high. We have encountered a medium-size division that subscribed to 250 different publications, and large companies that spent large sums on on-line data bases. In several cases these investments were poorly justified. A methodical process of source evaluation forces the company to look into the real value of sources of information.

The usefulness of a human or published source consists of the following points:

Relevance
Reliability
Depth of coverage
Uniqueness
Availability of alternate sources

Relevance. A source is useful if it provides data about the targets set by the BI system. This point escapes some corporations that subscribe to expensive and irrelevant sources out of sheer inertia. The element of relevance should serve as a test to the acquisition and maintenance of sources.

Reliability. Source reliability is derived through the process of keeping a record of data provided by each source and analyzing them for posterior validity. This procedure enables the determination of the extent to which a source provides good information over time.

If a source is new, and a track record has not yet been established, reliability can tentatively be estimated by asking the following questions: (1) How is the source motivated? Is the motivation out of revenge, money, or friendship? Not all motives imply the same reliability. Naturally, friendship is the best motive, revenge the worst. (2) What are the characteristics of the source? Human sources have personal characteristics; published sources have public ones. Prestigious sources are more reliable than gossip newspapers and prestigious people are more reliable in general than gossipers. Commonsense analysis of major characteristics can serve, for lack of hard data, as a basis for evaluation of reliability.

Depth of coverage. A newsmagazine usually covers a broad range of topics with little depth. A specialty publication (a trade newsletter, for example) covers a specific topic with great depth. Depth of coverage typically relates inversely to usefulness: The broader the coverage the less useful the source for intelligence purposes.

Uniqueness of coverage. Unique coverage means that the source specializes in providing information about a particular area and that there are no other sources that could provide the same information or the same perspective on the data. Uniqueness may apply to both field and published sources. In published sources it is very common to see specialized newsletters that cover very narrow and specific areas not covered by any other publications. Similarly, some field sources are unique in the information they provide. Of course this may pose a problem in evaluating the reliability of the source and the data it yields.

Alternate sources. If you can get the same data from substitute sources, the usefulness of the source under question declines. This competitive factor relates closely to the uniqueness of coverage. Unique coverage usually comes from a source with no good substitutes. The question of substitutes also involves cost considerations.

Summary: Usefulness of Sources

The five factors composing the overall usefulness of a source appear at the bottom of the source profile form in Figure 7–2. The

Figure 7–2. Source profile form.

```
                                         Date _____

Name _____

Address _____·_____

                                         Primary _____
                                         Secondary _____
General Description:


List below any unique topics or targets covered:


If field source—
Frequency of contact _____

If publication—
Frequency of issue: Daily _____ Weekly _____ Monthly _____
   Other (specify) _____

Cost _____

Comments:


Collector _____
_____

Usefulness: Relevance _____ Reliability _____

            Depth of coverage _____

            Uniqueness _____

            Alternate sources _____
```

form is the cornerstone of the source files that should be compiled and maintained by the BI unit. These files enable the BI unit to measure performance of its sources.

Similar to the "data usefulness" section, which appears at the bottom of the field intelligence report (Figure 5–7), the components of source usefulness can be measured on a scale using H, M, and L for high, medium, and low scores, or using a scale from 1 to 5. The overall judgment of source usefulness should serve as the rational basis for purging sources. The purge should be conducted periodically by the BI unit after consulting with the collector. This rational treatment of information purchasing is definitely one of the greatest fringe benefits of a formal BI system.

Final Word: From Evaluation to Analysis

The evaluation of data is the final technical stage in the intelligence process. An evaluated piece of data becomes information; it is no longer just raw. Evaluation itself, however, does not transform the data into input for decisions. This last processing step is the realm of analysis.

This takes us back to the chapter on critical intelligence needs, where we first discussed analysis. The analytical framework of business strategy is difficult to separate from any step in the BI process. It underlies the determination of what data to collect, it serves in the background of evaluating significance and relevance of data, and it figures again after the evaluation is completed. Thus, a theoretical perspective on strategy is required to make a preliminary determination of what of the multitude of facts around us is relevant to our company, and it is then required again to put the facts into a meaningful picture of the environment.

Unfortunately, we cannot hope to do justice to the complex topic of analysis in a single chapter. Several books are needed to cover the subject seriously. We therefore move from the evaluation stage to the storage and dissemination stage. We will return to the *management* of the analysis stage in the chapter on organizational structure.

8

The Intelligence Audit

The intelligence audit should be the first step in reorganizing the BI system or implementing a new one. The audit is a diagnostic tool. It is used to obtain data about aspects of the organization that are important to the establishment of the BI system. To design a sound business intelligence system, it is important to first conduct an audit in order to obtain answers to the following questions:

1. *What intelligence is needed by users?* Based on the results of the intelligence audit you can establish (1) user interest profiles for the dissemination of intelligence reports and (2) a list of targets for intelligence collection.

2. *What intelligence information is already available?* The intelligence audit reveals what intelligence data and sources are already available within the organization and where they are located.

3. *Who can serve as collectors of information?* The audit determines who in the organization has access to what sources of information— either published or field sources. This knowledge is used to establish a list of potential information that can be obtained from various departments and individuals within the firm.

4. *Who are the firm's experts on various topics of interest to the intelligence analyst and intelligence user?* The audit provides a list of

experts who can be consulted when the industry, competition, or technological environment is analyzed.

5. *What are the existing methods of communication of information in the organization?* Formal and informal methods of communication can provide means of communicating intelligence data by the collection network.

6. *What is the status of the firm's business intelligence operations?* What are the resources available for business intelligence, such as libraries, staff, and computer system? How do users evaluate the business intelligence system in terms of its usefulness? Is the system adequate for the company's needs? How would users want to change the business intelligence operation?

The audit may be conducted using a set of questionnaires (Figures 8–2 through 8–4), especially designed to obtain answers to the above questions. Our experience has shown, however, that audit interviews can be much more effective than questionnaires in eliciting needed detail and providing useful insights into the true operations of the system. During a face-to-face conversation, interviewees are apt to provide much richer information than through a written questionnaire, partly because an interview allows for immediate follow-up and clarification of detail, and partly because many people may be reluctant to answer long questionnaires. Figure 8–1 is a guide for conducting the audit interview.

As Figure 8–1 indicates, interview questions relate to the interviewee's role as an intelligence user and supplier.

Questions about the interviewee's role as an intelligence user include:

- Questions about types of decisions made by the interviewee
- Questions about the type of data used to support decisions
- Questions about the ways the data reach the interviewee, frequency of data transmission, sources of data, extent to which data need further processing before becoming useful for the decisions in question
- Questions about gaps in intelligence, areas where more intelligence is needed, important targets (CINs), and desired frequency and form of transmission

Figure 8–1.   The intelligence audit interview guide.

1. Before beginning each audit interview, cover the following points.
      The purpose of the study and the interview process.
      At the end of the interview the interviewee will have an opportunity to review and clarify his/her comments.

2. During the interview, explore the following topics. (Not all topics have to be covered; questions depend on the function of the individual interviewed.)
      What are your major responsibilities?
      To whom do you report?
      With what groups in the organization do you regularly interface?
      What decisions do you make? What reports do you write?
      What information do you need for your decisions? For your reports?
      What is the most useful information you receive? From whom?
      How does the information get to you?
      What are your contacts in the industry (such as suppliers, competitors, trade shows)? Are they sources of information?
      Do you get raw data or complete reports, or both?
      How would you rate the information you receive with respect to: Adequacy? Validity? Reliability? Timeliness? Volume?
      Are there experts on competitive and other topics within the organization whom you consult?
      Do you supply information to others in the organization? Whom?
      What changes could be made to help you get better intelligence?
      Is there anything else you would like to mention?

Questions about the interviewee's role as an intelligence supplier:

- Questions about the person's contacts outside the company, such as with suppliers, professional colleagues, and competitors, and what information they supply
- Questions about how the interviewee shares this information with others in the organization

It is worthwhile to note that most of those interviewed will fall into either of two categories: net users of intelligence and net providers of information. The first category includes decision-makers, those whom the system typically serves, mostly with strategic intelligence. They may include top management, the marketing department, other department heads, staff planners, competitive analysts, product managers, and line managers. Although all of them supply information, all in all they are the major consumers of intelligence information. Thus, they are called net users. Others in the organization have more limited information needs, usually for tactical information, but may be able to supply a wealth of information. They are the net suppliers and include salespeople, purchasing agents, the service staff, field engineers, and so on.

The interviews with net users and net suppliers will proceed differently. It is imperative to thoroughly interview net users regarding their information needs and how they use information because their input is essential to determine intelligence needs, targets, and priorities for the system as a whole. The interview with net suppliers, on the other hand, should concentrate on their sources of information and how they pass along the information they obtain.

The person conducting the audit interview should be prepared for the fact that many decision-makers do not possess ready insight into their own information needs. This is an additional reason why "canned" answers, as are required by using a written questionnaire, fail to elicit the desired responses. It is therefore the role of the BI specialist to elicit from the executive a sound understanding of the intelligence support he or she needs for decision making, and to obtain responses in terms of targets and priorities, communication blocks, the use of sources, and so on. It may also be advisable to distribute a preinterview questionnaire that will prepare the executive for the types of questions and information the BI specialist will be looking for.

Another experience we have had is with the wealth of after-thought communication from interviewees. In general, the interview stirs a lot of initial interest among the corporate decision-makers, and this interest translates into follow-up comments and afterthoughts by the executives interviewed. The BI specialist will do well to encourage the phenomenon by suggesting to the interviewees to think about the questions and their answers, and to urge them to return with additional insights.

It is important to plan the interview process in advance. First, the scope of the audit should be determined. Will it be conducted on a company-wide basis? Will it be carried out on a division-by-division basis? Will only some divisions be audited? The answer depends on whether you currently have or plan to establish a system for the whole company. It also depends on whether your company is so large that a comprehensive audit of the total organization becomes unwieldy. You may also wish to conduct the audit in only one of the divisions or departments first, draw your conclusions, learn from the process, and then proceed with the audit elsewhere. Next, careful consideration should be given to who is put on the interviewing list. All important users of intelligence should be included, especially if their information needs are different from each other's. Department heads are very important, not only as users, but also as providers of a good overview on how things are done within the department, its relation to other departments, and the main patterns of intra- and interdepartmental communication. As for net suppliers of information, there is no need to interview every salesperson, everyone in the purchasing department, or every engineer. A representative sample will do. Usually with the help of someone within the target department or functional area it is possible to pinpoint those people who are known to be the more vigorous collectors and disseminators of information.

The audit calls for about one hour to be set aside for each interview with a key user of intelligence, and approximately half that for collectors of intelligence. It is wise to be flexible and bend the schedule if an interview proves particularly useful. Similarly we sometimes find that an interview may be cut short after ten minutes if the person has nothing of value to contribute. Sometimes, as we go along, the list of those yet to be interviewed may shrink or expand. It will expand when interviewees mention someone not on your list who could be a valuable source of information, and will shrink if you find that certain departments do not yield useful information.

If through the interviews you cannot reach everyone you would like to contact, or if you would initially like to have only sketchy feedback regarding the audit questions, you may use the audit questionnaires to obtain information.

Each questionnaire contains questions addressing a particular area of interest included in the full audit. The questionnaire in Figure 8–2 is used to identify those already officially involved in the collection of information and those who serve as intelligence analysts or analysts in related areas. Such a questionnaire will have a limited circulation and will usually go to a manager within every department. Figure 8–3 is a questionnaire aimed at uncovering the existing methods of information transmission in the organization. The results from this questionnaire are used to tailor an intelligence dissemination system, piggybacking on already established channels of communication. Figure 8–4 presents an outline for a survey that will uncover net information suppliers, that is, departments and individuals that are mentioned more often as providers of intelligence data to others in the firm. The questionnaire can also be used in compiling a list of experts within the organization. Such findings are helpful in the formation of networks, assigning of collection responsibilities, and staffing various intelligence committees. Figure 8–4 can pinpoint specific sources of information, especially field information, and their collectors, who are sometimes referred to as "gatekeepers" of information and typically have good access to outside intelligence data.

Should the audit be conducted by the company's own personnel or by an outside consultant? There are advantages and disadvantages to either. Not everyone interviewed will talk openly about subjects such as communication bottlenecks, poor quality of information provided, or inadequate staffing. Often, an outside consultant can draw out reluctant interviewees to air their grievances and conduct frank views about the matter at hand because the consultant may more readily be perceived as an impartial listener. The use of an outside consultant may also serve to highlight the seriousness of the endeavor and will therefore elicit more sincere and thorough information. On the other hand, someone from within the organization may have more knowledge of the individuals involved and may be able to put them at ease. The decision whether to use an outsider or insider will thus depend upon such factors as the degree of politicization of the corporation, the general atmosphere regarding open discussions and criticism, and also the expertise of available interviewers. As long as the advocates of the BI program are aware of

Figure 8–2. Existing staff resources useful for business intelligence.

---

1. Is there anyone in your office, division, or company assigned to collect intelligence? Please list names and telephone numbers.

   a.
   b.
   c.
   d.

2. Is there anyone in your office, division, or company who performs industry or competitive analysis functions? Please list names and telephone numbers.

   a.
   b.
   c.
   d.

3. If there is no one who is currently performing competitive analysis, who do you think should be given this responsibility? Why?

4. Do you have a market research department?
   in the division_____in the company_____

5. Are there other groups involved in economic analysis, issues analysis, industry analysis, etc.? Please list.

   a.
   b.
   c.
   d.

Figure 8–3. Identifying channels of communication for BI.

1. Does your department or do people within the department submit any formal reports such as call reports, field inspection reports, trip reports?

   If YES, please describe each report briefly and indicate to whom and by whom they are submitted.

2. How do you ordinarily transmit information to others in the division?

   _____ written memos or letters
   _____ telephone calls
   _____ voice messages
   _____ electronic mail
   _____ formal meetings
   _____ informal meetings
   _____ other_____

   Which of the above do you use most often? _____
   For what types of information? _____

3. Do you transmit information to other divisions? _____

   If YES, how?

4. Do you have a formal system for transmitting intelligence? _____

   If YES, please describe.

Figure 8–4. Identifying intelligence flow patterns.

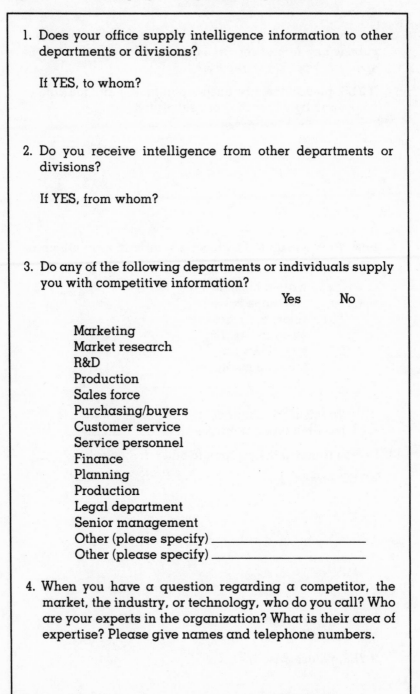

1. Does your office supply intelligence information to other departments or divisions?

   If YES, to whom?

2. Do you receive intelligence from other departments or divisions?

   If YES, from whom?

3. Do any of the following departments or individuals supply you with competitive information?

	Yes	No
Marketing		
Market research		
R&D		
Production		
Sales force		
Purchasing/buyers		
Customer service		
Service personnel		
Finance		
Planning		
Production		
Legal department		
Senior management		
Other (please specify) _____		
Other (please specify) _____		

4. When you have a question regarding a competitor, the market, the industry, or technology, who do you call? Who are your experts in the organization? What is their area of expertise? Please give names and telephone numbers.

these factors, they can take the corrective steps to advance the prospects of a successful audit.

Final Word

An audit should not be undertaken unless there is a commitment on the part of management to proceed soon after the audit has taken place with the establishment of a BI system or improvement of the existing BI process. The reason is obvious. The audit introduces the idea of a business intelligence system to many in the organization. By its nature, it raises expectations that management intends to improve the BI function. All too often surveys such as the audit are not followed by action. The result may be cynicism and apathy. The success of a business intelligence operation relies entirely on the active participation of everyone in the firm. If the beginning is inauspicious, if the audit is perceived as a road leading to nowhere, management may face an uphill battle in later implementing a successful BI system.

9

Storage and Dissemination

The chapter deals with the storage and dissemination of information in the BI system, whether manual or computer based.

Storage

A storage system is essential for the business intelligence process. Without an adequate means of storing and retrieving data, the painstaking collection of many bits and pieces of information becomes a useless task. Intelligence data must be accumulated over time in order for the data to have any long-term strategic utility. If the information is not available for later use in putting together the competitive puzzle, its value is limited to immediate conclusions that can be drawn from each discrete piece of information.

Intelligence data are thus especially difficult to manipulate and use, without the availability of a highly organized and accessible storage system. This is because of the nature of intelligence information, which is such that:

Most useful intelligence information is in textual form. Although some intelligence information is numerical, such as financial statements, pricing information, and cost information, most intelligence appears in textual form, which is a much less structured and compact form than numerical data. It may include a description of the competitor's product line, a list of its plants and their locations, and descriptions of manufacturing equipment and processes. The information will also consist of data about management, their background, the organizational structure of the competitor; textual information about the marketing practices of the competitor and its engineering capabilities; and information about competitive moves and future plans.

Most information is fragmented and from multiple sources. Most of the information collected about competitors, and in general about the external environment, appears as bits and pieces and comes from many different sources. To compile an intelligence portrait of the competition, all the fragments have to be categorized, collated, and related to each other.

Much of the data is emanative and must be related to be of value. Not only are intelligence data fragmented, but many of the developments in the competitive environment cannot be understood outside the context of the stream of events that led to their occurrence. Thus, much of the information, especially information coming from the field, is emanative, and in order to understand its full implication, it has to be related to what has preceded it, or to other events that influence the interpretation of the information.

Much of the information has time value. Much of the intelligence information has time value and therefore requires prompt action. Action may vary from the quest for additional information to clarify the situation, to the generation of an intelligence report, to a tactical move designed to counter competitor moves, to a strategic reorientation of the company.

These characteristics of intelligence data translate into the four basic requirements for a storage system:

1. The system must permit the storing and retrieving of *textual* information.
2. The system must permit the storage and manipulation of *large* amounts of data.

3. The system must facilitate the storage and retrieval of data by *multiple keys* so that bits of pieces can be related to each other.
4. The system must provide information on a *timely basis*.

With the advent of fast and sophisticated computer systems, ample low-cost electronic storage, and the availability of text-oriented data base management systems, more and more companies are converting their manual storage and retrieval methods to highly developed computerized systems. This trend is taking place because a computerized storage and retrieval system provides the best solutions to the four requirements above. This chapter will therefore emphasize the implementation of a computerized business intelligence system.

A good storage system, however, does not necessarily need to be computerized, although computer technology not only facilitates the task of storage and retrieval, but also enables analysts and other users to put data to use in ways that are otherwise impossible. It also provides several other advantages (discussed later in this chapter), beyond simple storage and retrieval, that can enhance the operation of the BI system as a whole.

How do most conventional storage systems look? While conventional manual storage systems vary to a degree, they all rely on paper files. Paper-based storage systems range from stacks of documents strewn at random all over the office to a sophisticated filing system with indexing and cross-referencing. They may be highly organized and centralized, as in the corporate business library, or may consist of any number of files that individuals maintain in their own offices.

An intelligence audit at one of our clients, a company in the automotive supply business, included an evaluation of their methods of intelligence data storage. While the audit revealed deficiencies in the way information was collected, the number of sources covered, and the use of information, we were impressed to note that a central "competitive library" had been established for use by the marketing department, staff planners, line management, and top management. The library included a file for each major competitor and several topic files. However, a more thorough analysis of a sample of library files was very instructive. It revealed that some files were empty, others contained very little information, yet others included large quantities of sporadic information. The files contained competitors' ads torn out of magazines, news articles, product catalogs, price lists, and a few field intelligence reports, most of them undated.

Given these results we began asking people to show us the files that they maintained in their offices, and which included competitive information. It came as no surprise that many did maintain very thorough files with a lot of interesting and useful information. Even the general manager of the company was guilty of hoarding competitive information, especially about one fast-growing new entrant who had been gaining market share and had been perceived as a threat by many in the organization. The general manager himself had only a vague idea of the information in his file, since his secretary deposited most of the documents in it, often before he even read them.

This type of story unfortunately is encountered all too often. The example also points to the difficulty of establishing and maintaining a centralized repository of competitive information. In the case of the automotive supply company, it was the general manager, himself guilty of withholding data from the central library, who had proposed and encouraged the establishment of the library. It takes more than a decision to establish a library to create a useful working tool for users of intelligence.

Where a centralized business intelligence filing system exists, whether centralized on the corporate level or on the divisional level, it may be highly organized and accessible. This is especially true if the files are maintained by library personnel who have the skill, knowledge, and discipline in maintaining a library of information. Such a manual system will consist of topic files and competitor files referenced by a card catalog. Access to the files may be restricted and the checking out of materials or files may be controlled by the librarian.

Obviously, a computerized storage and retrieval system has many advantages over even the most sophisticated manual system. First, the most obvious reason for computerizing is to simplify the task of locating a particular document or piece of information. There are additional advantages. Once data are loaded into the computer, they can be searched from remote locations, whether from within the same facility or from across the country. Also, compared to a manual system, the computer offers more varied methods of searching for the desired information. When intelligence data are computerized, a user can search the data base for any key word or string of characters that appears in the text, or through any descriptive field. Computerization also provides a permanent storage medium. Once information is put on the system, it never tears, fades, discolors, or gets lost, as happens so often in manual filing systems.

Because the computer is such an important instrument for a successful business intelligence system, the remainder of the section on storage will be devoted to the discussion of the implementation of a computerized BI system.

Designing a Computerized BI System

The computer system for business intelligence may evolve together with the BI system as a whole, or it may be implemented later. In no case should the design and implementation of a computer system precede the planning and implementation of the complete business intelligence system. The nature of the computerized system will depend to a great extent on the structure of the business intelligence function. Thus, the scope of the BI system will determine the scope of the computerized data base. It will also be one determinant of the type of information to be stored in the computerized data base. The scope and the organizational structure of the BI activity, that is, whether it is centralized or decentralized, will determine in part who will have direct access to the system. These and other factors will determine the system configuration: how information will be stored, how data are to be entered, output modes, hardware and software requirements.

A large company, with a product line ranging from electronic products to communications, designed its business intelligence operations around a sophisticated homegrown computer system that was to serve the whole company by providing on-line access to competitive information. Unfortunately, the costly system ultimately failed. The reasons were not directly related to the computer system itself. The company had sophisticated computer capabilities and the system, from a technical point of view, was well designed. The problems that led to the demise of the computerized system lay elsewhere. They pertained to the complete disregard of the need to understand the organizational aspects of the business intelligence process in the context of the company's own organization and to the fact that no forethought was given as to how the computer could serve as a tool to enhance the BI function. The system, as it was designed, had competitor profiles compiled by corporate staff that were available on-line to everyone in the organization. The profiles proved to hold too little competitive intelligence for some, irrelevant intelligence for others, and the system's noninteractive nature frustrated all.

Of course, the availability of a particular technology, such as electronic mail, networked microcomputers, or a mainframe, may affect one's conception of how the business intelligence process should be translated into an organizational reality. In this case, the design of the computer system should take place *concurrently* with the planning of the total business intelligence function.

There are several important elements that should be considered when designing and implementing a computerized BI system. A discussion of these elements and how they should be evaluated follows.

Specifying the Scope of the System

One of the first steps in designing the business intelligence system is the determination of the scope of the system. Here, too, the scope of the data base has to be established by deciding what decision-making areas the system will support. Not all the decision-making areas for which the business intelligence system provides information need be included in the computerized system. For example, even though it may be the responsibility of the BI unit to provide information about merger candidates, it may be decided that data about such companies will not be on the system, either because the interest in such companies is transitory and short term, or because a limited number of users within the company will need to access such information. Similarly, the BI system may provide users with information about new markets and industries, but most of the information may be coming from outside vendors because of a lack of expertise or internal access to information in industries or markets in which the company has little day-to-day contact. It would therefore seem to make no sense to set up a data base and file structure to store the little information about such industries that is to be collected internally.

There are several reasons why it is important to determine the scope of information to be included in the data base. The scope will partly determine the elements of the system. Data structure will be determined by the areas of information on the data base. The areas of coverage will also determine the detail of information to be stored. For example, the data base may be structured differently if the information were used solely for the purpose of strategic intelligence than if information were also used for tactical decisions. Scope of coverage will also dictate whether the system will be used by a limited number of users or by many within the organization. This, in turn, will have implications for system design. A limited-use system may consist of a local microcomputer, while a system with a broad scope, serving many decision-making areas, will have to be hosted by a mainframe accessible to all potential users within the organization. Such a mainframe system can aid decision making in the crucial areas of (1) strategic planning, (2) identifying threats and opportunities, (3) mergers and acquisitions, (4) new product development, (5) entering new markets and industries, (6) establishing a new business, (7) R&D planning, and (8) tactical decisions.

Defining System Types

One of the areas where companies most differ regarding system design, and in fact, an area that almost solely defines the nature of the business intelligence computer system, is system type. A business intelligence computer system can be categorized by the type of information stored in its data base, and by implication, by how the system is used in the business intelligence process. System types are geared toward the following:

1. The storage and retrieval of raw data
2. The storage and retrieval of abstracts of raw data
3. The storage and retrieval of processed data
4. The storage and retrieval of intelligence reports and competitor profiles

Systems 1 and 2 are very similar in nature. Under system 1 raw data are stored as is. In system 2 the raw data undergo some initial processing in the form of abstracting. In either case, what is available on the system is raw information. With raw information on the data base, users, whether intelligence analysts or decision-makers, can browse through the data base to answer any question, general or specific. They can also use the system to keep track of environmental events, to compile intelligence reports on any topic, or to update competitor profiles. The availability of raw data on the computer gives flexibility and speed to the process of producing final intelligence from the initial raw data.

This is in great contrast to system type 4, where what is stored on the computer and available to users is the final intelligence, in other words the competitor profile or intelligence report. The value of such a system is limited. All it does, in fact, is replace typed intelligence reports with electronic reports. In our opinion, to establish a computer system that is limited to the *dissemination* of intelligence is to underutilize a very important tool for business intelligence and to invest scarce resources unwisely. The experience of the few companies that established such a system has shown small added value to the total BI process. System 3 lies somewhere in between. It is similar to type 4 in that the information stored in the data base is already processed information. For example, where systems 1 and 2 would store every piece of data that has arrived over a period of time regarding the product lines of the competitors, system 3 would include a detailed summary of all information about the competitors' product lines and recent changes in their product lines. Thus, the information is not integrated into a comprehensive intelligence report, as it would be under type 4, nor does it consist of many discrete, unrelated pieces of data.

Below are some further details about constructing a data base that conforms to each of the system types above.

Document/text storage and retrieval (raw data). Raw data may consist of field information, published information, or both. Whatever the source of the information, whether field data or published documents, for each element of raw data stored, the following information should be included in the data base record:

Source (complete reference)
Content
Reliability of the source
Validity score
Security/access restrictions

Storage and retrieval of abstracts. The problem with storing BI information in its raw form is that it is mostly qualitative in nature and consists of large amounts of data, sometimes requiring several clerical workers just to enter it. If a system is to be practical, the input should be of abstracts, not full-text documents. An abstract provides detailed information on the content of a document, and, in some cases, substitutes the document in meeting information needs. Abstracts include terms, events, processes, people, and companies that highlight the content of the document. Usually published information needs abstracting; field information rarely needs such treatment, mainly because each piece of field information is small and limited to one or two specific events. The storage of abstracts, not the full text of documents, brings with it a different set of requirements from the simple storage of raw data. Abstracting requires expert handling on its own. It must be performed by a knowledgeable person who can extract the essence of the document in a few key sentences without leaving out important information. The abstract must be accurate and concise and reflect as much as possible all the relevant information in the document. An abstracter must have knowledge of the subject matter, the areas of interest to users of the data base, and the capability to write well.

At one company, abstracting is a two-stage process. Several staff members within the business information unit read magazines and underline sentences and sections that contain relevant information. Professional abstracters then, based on the initial processing, prepare abstracts for the data base. This procedure makes the process very efficient. It also allows a group of knowledgeable intelligence staff people to concentrate on scanning magazines, while at the same time performing the initial step in the abstracting process, which requires, like scanning material, a high degree of knowledge of the subject matter. At the same time, it frees them from the burden of having to reformulate the material in a format appropriate for data base storage. Under this system, some material also arrives from other departments within the organization, already annotated and marked for extraction. Such articles are sent by senior executives, engineers, research personnel, and marketing and product managers.

It is interesting to note that most of the companies that we have polled who said they abstracted information for their intelligence data bases abstract information that might already be available on external commercial on-line data base systems. The reason these companies invest in the costly and time-consuming task of abstracting information is twofold. In-house abstracting allows them to present the information in a format geared to their own needs and convenient to their users. It also gives them the information on a more timely basis.

Storage and retrieval of processed data. Rather than storing every piece of data as it is captured, under this scheme information is periodically integrated into information already existing on-line.

Thus, information that has already undergone the first stages of analysis is available on the data base.

For example, one company, which faced several large and many small competitors, decided to structure its data base as a system type 3. Information about competitors was categorized into many different areas, such as product line, manufacturing capabilities, and management. Included within each category was a summary of relevant data that had been collected, together with an assessment of the information and its implications. These assessments were updated periodically as significant data were added to the summary.

Storage of intelligence reports and competitor profiles.   In this type of system only complete intelligence reports and competitor profiles are available on the data base. The system, in effect, serves as a vehicle for the dissemination of intelligence and nothing more. Of course, a system that primarily serves for the storage and retrieval of data does not preclude the availability of the intelligence reports on-line. These reports should become part of the permanent body of intelligence information available on the system.

Determining Output Requirements

Once the nature of the system is defined, and it has been decided whether it includes raw or processed data, it is important to outline how data will be entered, and who will access the system for information and how. Some of the questions that are considered below regarding the determination of system output go beyond the computer system itself and actually pertain to the total BI procedure.

Establishing users.   First it should be established who the system users are. There are two kinds of users: direct users and indirect users. Direct users are those who access the system directly. Indirect users are end-users who obtain the information through the services of others, typically a staff intelligence person. There are several advantages to limiting direct access to the system to intelligence staff only. First, efficient retrieval of information requires expertise that can be acquired through repeated use of the system. Occasional users do not develop the same knowledge and expertise in the use of the data base as the professional intelligence staff. Second, in terms of system and data security, system access through a limited number of terminals will provide fewer opportunities for security breaches.

Third, with requests for intelligence funneled through the intelligence staff, there is better control over the intelligence product, and the intelligence staff gain better understanding of the intelligence requirements of users in the organization.

It seems, however, that providing data base access to all authorized intelligence users outweighs the "advantages" listed above. The ability to browse through the system will give users a better idea of the types of intelligence available in the organization, thereby enhancing their ability to use information in their day-to-day decisions. And if every request for information has to pass through a staff intelligence unit, the demands on the unit will preclude it from doing anything but data base searches.

Identifying user needs. This step is actually part of the initial steps in designing a collection network. As mentioned in an earlier chapter, one of the tools for identifying user needs is the intelligence audit. The necessity of identifying user needs is mentioned here again to remind managers who are establishing an intelligence data base that not every piece of information that exists in the organization or that can be obtained should be put on the system. Although the data base can hold vast amounts of information, in order not to encumber the process of data entry, updating, and maintenance, only information directly related to user needs should be put on the system.

We are reminded of a client of ours who asked us to review their progress in establishing their business intelligence system. Being a company that had long relied on computer assistance for many of its operations, from inventory control and production scheduling to the monitoring of sales territories and running demand forecast models, one of their first steps in designing a BI system was to establish a data base. A group of managers met to discuss any relevant data bases that had already been in existence in the company and how they could be integrated into one intelligence data base. Through various intensive meetings the group, assisted by representatives from data processing, discussed the technical problems associated with integrating those data bases. Only after our intervention did they begin to first think about user needs and whether the existing data bases, which posed such a technical problem, would in fact be useful to anyone. A survey of users indicated that more than half of the data bases, which contained mostly numerical information, were dispensable.

Designing intelligence reports. The kinds of intelligence reports that will be generated by the system depend on user needs as determined by the intelligence audit. The intelligence reports that should be generated are not dependent on the computer system. An effort should be made to include in the computer data base all the information that will be needed in compiling the required reports. Of course, if intelligence reports, such as competitor profiles, are to be included on the system, the format has to be determined according to established user needs. (A more detailed discussion of intelligence reporting will be covered in the latter part of the chapter.)

We would like to mention here one aspect of the computer system that is related to the topic of reporting and dissemination. Most computerized BI systems provide on-line access to the user and the user is then capable of conducting his/her own data base search. Existing text-oriented software programs have in addition a feature that facilitates data base search strategies.

For example, a program called BASIS (TM by Information Dimensions, Inc.) has a program module, PROFILE, that provides the capability to save search strategies. Thus, if a certain type of search is performed regularly, the command sequence may be saved and later executed by a one-word command. Through the PROFILE module it is also possible to create a menu-oriented search approach.

These menus are most useful for persons who seldom use the data base. They need only select a letter from a list of possible alternatives shown on the screen and the menu will direct them through the search and provide the desired information.

Similarly, the text-oriented software INQUIRE (TM Infodata, Inc.) has a macro procedure language facility that allows the storage and execution of commands to provide standard, canned functions.

One may go even a step further and include on the system preprogrammed search strategies for broad questions. For example a preprogrammed question may be, "What is the marketing capacity of Company X?" The guidelines provided by the computer would be to search for key topics and index words relating to:

Distribution channel capacity
Field sales
Service
Technical sales experience
Advertising budget

Similarly, a question such as, "What is the capability of Company X to introduce new product Y next year?" will involve search for index words such as:

Company X
Financial capability
Production capability
Marketing capability
Technological capability
Regulatory
Product Y

Determining What Computer Systems Are Available

Hardware. It is unlikely that the company will invest in new computer hardware for the BI system alone. This is why it is important to find out what the options are for establishing the BI data base. The hardware available for hosting a software program for business intelligence varies depending on what hierarchical level of the organization is considered. Typically, in a large corporation there are three levels of information systems. The corporate level is the highest level of a corporation's information hierarchy: It is the MIS department that includes a mainframe. The second level addresses the divisional or departmental requirements of the corporation. It is usually an interactive, transaction-oriented environment. Minicomputers perform most of the processing at this level. The third level is the local level, which is the province of end-users. They use remote terminals or PCs to perform their own personal or departmental information processing.

Of the three levels the ones most often used for business intelligence computer support are the corporate MIS level with its mainframe, and the local level, typically with the use of a personal computer.

Microcomputers have limited use in supporting the business intelligence function. Their storage capacity is limited; their processing capability is circumscribed; they provide access to one person at a time (unless they are networked), and are usually limited to local users only. Needless to say, it is difficult to develop an extensive data base on a microcomputer. Furthermore, there are very few PC software programs that provide the necessary tools to manipulate the large amount of data involved in intelligence storage and retrieval.

On the other hand, mainframes are eminently suited for the task of intelligence storage and retrieval. They provide large storage capacity, can run complex software programs, and are accessible by many users simultaneously.

Software options. The problem with storing intelligence information is that it is mostly qualitative in nature, requiring text-oriented software that can handle sophisticated searches efficiently. Not many data base management software programs exist that answer these requirements. Most data base management systems are geared to numerical data and brief entries. There are, however, several text-oriented data base management systems on the market today. Practically all of them are geared to the mainframe, supermini, or mini-computers.

These programs, such as INQUIRE/Text and BASIS mentioned earlier, are text-oriented data base management systems that index each word in a document. This allows users to search a document for any word in the document, word roots or prefixes, words adjacent to each other, words within the same sentence, and words within a user-specified distance of each other. These programs are relatively user-friendly and provide much flexibility in redesigning the data base.

What software is available internally?   Few companies develop their own in-house text data base management software. With the commercial availability of sophisticated programs, it is simply not cost effective to do so. We do advise those who are interested in establishing an intelligence data base to check whether the company has acquired and is already using one of the commercial text-management systems. Several of our clients found out that a system that they were considering was already installed and used by another department. One client was able to begin using a data base management system that had been in use for two years by the legal department for storage and retrieval of legal documents. Intelligence staff then benefited from the expertise in system design and use accumulated by the legal staff.

What existing data bases can be useful?   Consider carefully what existing data bases may contain information that should be put on the new intelligence data base. These may include a small data base that exists on someone's microcomputer or a large one that has been set up by one of the departments for its own use. If it is a very specialized data base it may remain separate, but information it contains should be made available to intelligence users. In some cases, it may be more desirable to link relevant data bases for ease of input, update, and use.

Establishing the Input

Determining method of data entry. The major problem with a full-text data base is getting the data into the system. First, they must be put into machine-readable form, then converted into a format required for loading. For published sources of data that are to be inputted as full-text documents, if there is a large volume of input, an optical character recognition (OCR) system can be used. It does, however, have severe limitations in the number and variety of type fonts and formats it can handle. Recently, character recognition equipment that uses artificial intelligence software that can scan virtually any typeset or typewritten document has become available. One such system is the Kurzweil Intelligent Scanning System, which can enter text into the computer system up to ten times faster than the best human keyboard operator. Other options for input are directly on-line, through a word-processing program, or magnetic media such as magnetic tape or diskette.

In addition to the mechanics of data input, a decision has to be made as to who will input the data. Data can be entered by BI staff or directly by collectors. The advantage of BI staff entering the information is tighter control over input and its quality. The advantage of collectors entering data directly is timeliness. As will be shown in the examples below, most companies have opted for input by BI staff. At one company the input scheme consists of both. Information is keyed in onto diskettes at the locations where it has been collected. The diskettes are then sent to the BI staff who load their content on the system and at the same time monitor the information for its viability and completeness.

These are some other elements that should be considered regarding input: First, determine processing of data, if any, before input. For example, published information may be abstracted and field information may be edited for clarity and consistency. Second, an input interface, such as input screens, should be designed. Last, establish information quality control procedures to ensure the quality of the information on the data base.

Determining what should be computerized and what should not. Often companies learn the hard way what should be computerized and what should not. Even if it is difficult to know in advance what will eventually prove most useful on the system, thought should be given at the planning stage to what information should be included and what should be refused. The questions to ask are: Will this particular information be more accessible if it is on the data base? Is the information available on a timely basis and in a useful format on a commercial data base? How specialized is the particular information? Will it have wide-ranging use or will it be needed by only one or two people for their own specialized work?

The reason there is a need to be selective in storing data on the system is neither a limitation on the amount of information that can be stored on the system nor a limitation on the processing capacity of the DBMS. Such systems can easily store millions of pages of text. The consideration is on the input side. The process of keying in information is labor intensive and thus the input phase can serve as a bottleneck to the whole system.

One company that set up a computerized business intelligence system had intended to include two types of information about some forty companies on its data base. One type consisted of competitive profiles of those 40 competitors. The other information consisted of "current events" pertaining to the same 40 companies. The intention was good, but very quickly current events became old history when the input clerk could not keep up with the onslaught of data. When the company reevaluated what was being put on the system, management realized that much of the needed current events information was available on-line externally and the current events aspect of the system was dropped.

Another company experienced a similar input problem. When a computerized intelligence system had just been installed, there had been a decision to put all archived competitive material onto the data base. Very soon management realized that the task was burdensome and in any case unnecessary, because older information was rarely accessed.

Fitting the System into the Organizational Structure

The computerized BI system should mirror the way the corporation and its business intelligence function are organized. The system should be fully integrated into the business intelligence process.

Thus, if the BI system is centralized, the computer system may be operated from the central business intelligence unit. The system itself may provide either raw intelligence or analyzed information, or both, depending on the considerations established when the system was designed. When the BI system is decentralized, the computer system can still be maintained centrally, but in all likelihood it will only provide intelligence data that the various business units can retrieve with which to conduct their own analysis.

Evaluating the System

Once you have determined the features you would like your BI computer system to have, you must evaluate the system design and the advantages of the various features in processing intelligence data. Alternative system configurations should be evaluated for their desirability and applicability to your unique situation. To help you in configuring your system, we list below the salient features of a computer system and their merits.

Storing and retrieval of textual information. When we discuss a computerized system for business intelligence, we are talking about a data base management system that will handle the storage and retrieval of textual data. Most of the DBMSs on the market today are not text-oriented but are designed to handle numerical data and limited textual information. There are, however, a few, specialized text-oriented DBMSs that enable the manipulation of text in a very efficient manner. These programs operate mainly on mainframe, supermini, and minicomputers. Ask yourself whether the DBMS you have picked can efficiently handle text-oriented information.

Storing and manipulating large amounts of data. The competitive environment is vast and complex and provides many fragments of data that have to be stored and manipulated. A good business intelligence storage system will facilitate the manipulation of these large amounts of data. Because of this requirement, sophisticated business intelligence systems have been established on mainframe computers. Those that are hosted on a microcomputer tend to be limited in scope and serve only one or a few users. Is your BI system vast in scope? Will it require the manipulation of large amounts of data? Do you follow any competitors and collect much information about them? Will the system support many users with many different needs? If so, you will need to establish a system that will facilitate the manipulation of large amounts of data.

Storing and retrieval by multiple keys. In intelligence work it is essential to be able to retrieve information through many different paths. This is important when one needs to answer questions that cut across subject areas. For example, one may need to answer a question such as, "Which companies are developing new imaging devices in medicine?" To answer the question, one might need to look into files that contain information about certain companies and files that contain information about the field of imaging devices. That may require a certain amount of cross-referencing between files to make the retrieval job manageable. A sophisticated data base management system provides easy storage and retrieval by multiple keys to enable access through many different paths so that the desired cross-referenced material is retrieved. Here you should ask yourself whether the intelligence questions your decision-makers ask are complex in nature and require retrieval through multiple paths. It is our experience that no matter how simple the intelligence requirements, this feature of the computerized data base is one of the more helpful ones.

Easy and timely access and retrieval. The "timeliness" required of the information depends on the information itself. Information accumulated for the compilation of a strategic plan with a five-year horizon does not require immediate action. Its "time horizon" is long. From the standpoint of timeliness, a manual filing system may serve adequately such information needs. Decisions designed to counter current competitive moves, such as price changes, product enhancements, or changes in advertising and promotion, require that information about such events be made available much sooner. The time horizon for this information is short. A manual filing system does not facilitate the detection of such short-term changes in the environment. On the other hand, once such information is loaded onto a computerized data base, browsing for current developments or retrieving information pertaining to a particular event or topic is made easy and timely. The question to ask here is about the time horizon of your information requirements.

Accessibility by multiple users and remote access. If there are to be more than a few users for the storage system who may need the same information on an ongoing basis, the system should provide easy accessibility to various users simultaneously. In a manual system, a clipping, a competitor file, or a technical report that has been checked out is not available to other users at the same time. A microcomputer will also provide only limited accessibility on a one-by-one basis, unless the microcomputers have been networked and provide access to a common data base. A mini- or mainframe computer can provide simultaneous access to many users in many different and remote locations. This is one distinct advantage of a centralized computer system over manual files: its ability to service users in remote locations. This not only brings information to those who might otherwise not have information for their decision making. It also affords economies of scale in information use, saves costs by providing a shared resource, and increases efficiencies in information use. How many users who will need to have direct access to the intelligence data base will your system have? Are they all located in one building? Are they in remote geographical locations? Does the system serve several business units in several different locations? The answers to these questions will determine whether you will want to have a data base accessible by multiple users on-line.

Easy scanning. Scanning or browsing through a data base is important because it lets users stay on top of current events and enables them to get a quick rundown on the existing information about a particular target or topic. A computerized system that can search through and retrieve large amounts of data very quickly and that provides multiple paths for accessing the data base makes the scanning task efficient and timely, and in all likelihood will uncover most of the information pertaining to the desired topic. A manual system consisting of paper files makes a comparable search difficult to accomplish. In fact, most manual files discourage users from browsing altogether and so, ultimately, the collected intelligence data are less useful than if they were computerized. How important is browsing to your users and analysts?

Protecting against data loss and misfiling of information. Once a document, abstract, or field intelligence report is put on an electronic data base there is no danger of misplacing the item. Numerous users may look at the item, download it to their PC, or make a hard copy of it without touching the "original" stored document. Does your manual storage system have appropriate safeguards against loss of documents? If not, can you rectify the problem or are you better off with a computerized system?

Encouraging system use.   Whether a storage system is manual or computerized it should be user-friendly. Of course, the degree of user friendliness is bounded by the storage technology. Manual files may discourage regular use for several reasons. Manual files may be bulky. You may have to go to the physical location where they are stored, such as the library. In manual systems there is also a limitation on the cross-referencing that realistically may be achieved. Any problems that may exist with encouraging use of a computer system stem from a different source. Typically they are related to how user-friendly the data base access and search methods are. The more expertise required to use the system, the less user-friendly it is and the fewer the people who will take the time and trouble to learn the system intricacies. If it takes frequent and extensive system use to know its ins and outs, very few occasional users will access a data base themselves. In such a case, the professional BI staff will end up doing all data base searches directly. If you have decided on a computerized system, is it user-friendly? What are the features that will make it accessible to the occasional user? Alternatively, will you limit system access to the BI professional?

Minimizing time and cost of data entry.   In a manual filing system, the cost of inputting relates mostly to the need to cross-reference information, which is a time-consuming job. In a computerized system, the major cost arises from the need to convert printed information into machine-readable form. This is achieved by entering information through a word-processing system or a PC, directly on-line, or through an optical character recognition system. Except for the last method, all input methods are labor intensive. Input time can be minimized by abstracting information rather than entering whole documents onto the data base. Input may also be made efficient if special input screens are designed for guided input and editing operations. Have you considered the question of input when deciding what information should go on the system? Have you thought about the sources of your data? For example, if much of the information to be put on the system originates in field intelligence reports that are handwritten, they will have to be prepared for input, since OCR does not yet scan handwriting.

Facilitating gathering and updating of data.   An electronic medium such as a computer data base enables more than storage and retrieval of information. The system provides the means of remote entry of data and thereby serves as a means of gathering data from a remote location. In this way, direct entry of information from remote locations, such as branch sales offices, can serve as one means of communicating data from the collection network. Is the field a major source of information for your BI program? Will direct access facilitate the collection of data from the field?

For a computer system to be successful in the long run, it is essential to establish criteria for long-term system evaluation. The most important issue is whether the system answers user needs, whether users are the decision makers or the BI staff. Does the data base contain complete information? Does it cover the areas of interest to users? Is the information in a format desired by users? Is the information detailed enough? Is data base search easy or difficult, especially for the occasional user? Does the system facilitate browsing and the answering of intelligence questions? You can best answer these questions only after the system has been operating for some time. Then user feedback can be obtained, including suggestions for improvement.

Training

When dealing with computerized data base management systems, we are dealing with technology that needs to be understood both by those who will structure the system and maintain it and by those who will use the system as a tool in their day-to-day work. It is therefore important to establish several levels of training regarding the system.

Designing and implementing the system. Vendors of text-oriented data base management software provide training geared to two kinds of audiences: (1) the user, on how to use the system, and (2) the system professional, on how to design and develop the data base. Typically, a training program on system design will include information about using the software, writing data definition language, indexing strategies, instituting security measures, building and loading a thesaurus, and updating a data base. A program may also include instruction on developing menu-driven interfaces to the data base and designing formatted reports.

Inputting information.   Support staff who will be charged with data input should be taught how to use specially designed input screens for entering and updating data.

Accessing and using the system.   Users will be informed about the data base structure and content so that they know what information is available on the system. They will learn whether the data base contains raw data, abstracts, field information, and/or intelligence reports. They will also be taught data base search strategies and procedures for accessing the information.

Computerized BI Systems Now in Use

A survey among large companies shows, not surprisingly, that many of the computerized intelligence systems tend to have similar features and could easily be categorized according to the several system features discussed above. Examples of some of the systems will be described below. It should be noted that the longest running systems in our survey have been in operation for three years; the shortest, for two months. Thus, many of the systems are in their first stages of evolution and may not provide a long-term perspective.

The scope of the system varies from company to company, but all systems concentrate heavily on competitive information. Some have added areas of coverage, such as markets and acquisition candidates. The most distinct difference is found in system types. Systems divide into two categories: those hosting raw data and those hosting processed information. Only one older and now-defunct system contained competitive profiles exclusively. In one aspect all systems are alike. No matter what the method of data input, all data, whether collected by BI staff or coming from the field, are inputted onto the data base by BI staff. In all cases the systems have the capability of incorporating on-line input from remote sites, but because of a uniform need for data quality control, information is directly controlled by BI staff. All the systems described below operate on either a mainframe or minicomputer and are centralized organizationally; that is, they either serve the total organization, where business units are sufficiently close in needs, or serve a group of strategically related business units (see chapter on organizational structure).

Case I

A chemical manufacturer has a centralized business intelligence department, the business information group, that serves as a central clearinghouse of intelligence data for the whole company. The group is responsible for the maintenance and operation of an intelligence data base that is run with a text-oriented data base management system on its mainframe computer. The system is used to store raw intelligence data. The data consist of field intelligence information in its original form and abstracts of published information. The original published documents are filed conventionally or put on microfilm.

The data base contains two broad classes of information: about the company's markets and about the competition. The market category includes information about present market conditions and major clients. The competitor category encompasses complete information for a competitor profile and information about competitive moves such as competitor product introductions and product features; other strategic moves, such as changes in pricing, underbidding by competitors in particular markets, openings of new plants, and acquisitions, are also included.

Occasionally information is purged from the data base, not for lack of computer storage space, but to eliminate information that is known not to be factual. This turns out to be mostly field information that is later found to represent rumors only.

Originally, the system was designed so that all of the company's offices across the country had the capability to access the system on-line. Although offices do have the technical capability to input information directly into the system, it was decided, because of concerns about the quality of information, to control the input by keying it in centrally at the business information group. The security of the system is maintained through a controlled allocation of terminals to users rather than through the use of passwords. The decision not to use passwords was based on the perception of their relative ineffectiveness and that they might only discourage use of the system by the occasional user.

The data base is available not only to the business information group, but to any user who has access to a terminal. Although the manufacturer provides user training along with the program, it has not been feasible to provide extensive training for all potential users. The group has therefore devised a simple one-page guide on how to use the system; it covers two simple basic commands for searching through the data base.

Users, however, tend not to do their own data base searching. Rather, they will call one of the analysts at the group and have them do the search. This pattern of use, we have found, is very common. Even though the system may be user-friendly, if there is a specialist within the company in data base search, whether internal or external data bases are concerned, users will tend to go to the specialist rather than learn the intricacies of the system. Thus, in the case of the chemical company, the business information group generates two kinds of intelligence reports: One type consists of compilation of data that result from the data base search. This task is usually designed to answer narrow and very specific questions. Mostly, however, the group produces, on demand, complete intelligence reports that are tailored to user needs. These special studies are made available to other users who may have an interest in them. The only "off the shelf product" produced by the group are competitor profiles, which are maintained and updated on the system.

Scope:	Market, competitors
Type:	Raw data—abstracts and field reports
Users:	Business information group (BIG) and any users
Hardware:	Mainframe
Software:	Leading text DBMS
Input:	Local by BIG through on-line keying
BI Reports:	Competitor profiles, custom intelligence reports, data base searches on specific narrow questions
Organization:	Centralized

Case II

A biotechnology company, much smaller in size then the above chemical corporation, has also set up its computerized intelligence system as a central system. The system has been structured differently. Rather than purely raw data, it holds processed information. The data base contains information, summarized by categories, about several hundred companies active in the area of biotechnology. It was begun as a file on a word-processing system. Soon, however, the amount of material outgrew the capabilities of the system and a solution to the expanding data base was found in one of the leading text-oriented DBMSs that now runs on a VAX minicomputer. The data base is slanted toward information about research carried out by other companies and is used to track competing projects or to identify candidates for joint ventures or acquisitions. Accordingly, the emphasis is on data about companies' R&D projects, the nature of the projects and their stage of development, and joint ventures that have been formed by other companies. The reports produced by the intelligence staff revolve mostly around products, but more comprehensive competitor profiles are also generated on demand. The sources of information are primarily secondary since field information is only occasionally conveyed to the library staff responsible for maintaining the data base. Each category of information is assigned a field in the data base, and since the system has been evolving, new fields are constantly added to the data base definition.

Scope:	Competitors, product-related intelligence
Type:	Processed data
Users:	Intelligence staff and librarians
Hardware:	Minicomputer
Software:	Leading text DBMS
Input:	Local on-line
BI Reports:	Competitor profiles, product-based reports
Organization:	Centralized

Case III

The computerized system that this large diversified manufacturer is now using has evolved to its current configuration over a period of time. For several years the company had employed one person whose sole responsibility was to scan a list of trade and technical publications, abstract the relevant articles, and input them onto a relational data base. Eventually, as the data base grew in size and sophistication, and as the number of people who tapped into the system increased, it could not accommodate the need for large quantities of text and the varied uses of information. A new system was set up, using a text-oriented DBMS. The data base now contains field information, too. The system is mostly used by the staff of the corporate business intelligence department. The BI staff has made an effort to familiarize potential users with the system and its features so as to encourage direct access and use. Although the BI department has been growing, because it serves a large and diversified organization, it cannot catch up with the demand for its services and encourages individuals within the business units to take advantage of the system's information directly. But the biggest obstacle to widespread use of the system has been training. The BI staff has made an effort to teach people how to use the system. Most users, however, prefer to call the BI department and ask them to do the data base searching. Because of this, one person in the BI department has become the expert on system access and search and is engaged in data retrieval full-time.

As mentioned above, the company is a diversified corporation with business units operating in diverse markets and industries. For this reason it was decided that the data base, which is maintained and managed centrally, would include raw data. It was felt that a data base of raw data would best suit the company's needs. The logic was that even though the BI department was large by current standards for BI units, it could not accommodate all user needs if its staff had to process and analyze every piece of information received. Also, because the needs of the business units were not uniform, it appeared that unstructured data would best answer everyone's needs. Thus, storage of raw data would provide the system with the greatest flexibility and the ability to accommodate new needs and changes in coverage.

Remote access terminals are only allowed to read the data base. Field information or printed material that is sent to the BI department from collectors in the organization is entered on a PC and then loaded onto the system.

Scope:	Competitors
Type:	Raw data—abstracts, field reports; competitor reports
Users:	Mostly BI group
Hardware:	Mainframe
Software:	Leading text DBMS
Input:	Local—data keyed in on PC
Organization:	Centralized collection, decentralized analysis

Case IV

A company in the aerospace business has designed a business intelligence data base that serves all of its divisions. Initially, input

was allowed through modems from any division and centrally at the
BI unit, where staff entered information using a Kurzweil reader and
word processors from which the data were then loaded onto the data
base. To better control the input and quality of information, remote
locations now send in diskettes with data that are loaded onto the
system by the BI staff. The system does not include raw data per se
but structured information; that is, information about competitors
that has already been evaluated, categorized, and analyzed. The data
base is broken down into fields, each representing an area within the
competitor profile. For example, one field contains information about
the competitor's manufacturing expertise, as perceived and evaluated
by people within the company. Another field includes financial
information and analysis of the competitor's financial standing. Additional information that is put on the system is about subcontractors
and suppliers, which is obtained from the purchasing department.
This supplier intelligence is used both for competitive assessment
and for the purpose of forming alliances with subcontractors.

Scope:	Competitors, subcontractors
Type:	Processed data
Users:	Anyone who has terminal
Hardware:	Mainframe
Software:	Leading text DBMS
Input:	Local—word-processing key-in and OCR
Organization:	Centralized

Dissemination

The final phase of the intelligence cycle is the dissemination of
intelligence to users. There are several questions that should be
considered at this phase of the intelligence cycle:

Who are the intelligence users and what are their needs?
What kind of reports should be generated and how often?
How should intelligence be disseminated to users?

Intelligence Users and Their Needs

Through the intelligence audit you will identify users and their
needs. Of course, the audit is the initial step that provides informa-

tion with which to begin designing the system. As the BI system evolves, additional users and needs will be identified and requirements for intelligence will undergo change.

What Reports Should Be Generated

Based on the identified user needs BI staff can design the needed reports. Intelligence reports can be classified in several ways. First, there are preestablished reports, which are generated on a regular basis and distributed to a predetermined list of users. At the other end of the spectrum are the user-requested reports that have no preexisting format, frequency, length, or contact. Typically, they would have a narrow focus and pertain to a limited number of questions. Sometimes, however, they can be of broad scope and require extensive research and analysis.

Another classification of intelligence reports concerns those generated for either operational or strategic purposes. Operational intelligence typically has a short horizon and requires immediate consideration. It will contain information about developments that management may want to counter immediately. Such intelligence will therefore be reported on a daily basis or as the information becomes available. Examples of operational intelligence include reports on competitor price changes, discounts and sales promotion, market analysis summaries, and significant announcements by competitors regarding intentions to increase capacity, enter a new market, or acquire another company.

Strategic intelligence will, in general, be reported on a monthly, quarterly, and annual basis. Such intelligence supports longer-term decisions and as such consists of the compilation of comprehensive information that has been accumulated over a period of time. Strategic reports may include a monthly compilation of key statistics, quarterly profiling of competitors, and annual analysis of market trends. Its primary use is in the preparation of proposals and strategic plans.

Strategic intelligence should be available to decision-makers early on in the planning process, otherwise it does not truly serve its purpose of providing information on which to base strategic decisions. Strategic intelligence reports should not merely be a neat package added to the strategic or marketing plan for the sake of completeness of presentation. It should serve as a working tool for management for the establishment of strategic direction.

Four generic reports cover the spectrum of reporting needs. They are summarized in Table 9–1.

Critical intelligence reports are designed to disseminate information quickly for immediate action. The report is short, descriptive, and specific, and contains very little analysis. It may consist of some collected piece of information that has undergone little processing. All too often a company's method of dissemination consists of reports that resemble the critical intelligence report. This format of focused, short, and descriptive reporting should be reserved for information that needs immediate action or alerts others to developments that may require action in the near future.

The situation report may be either strategic or operational in orientation. Its purpose is to alert decision-makers to competitor activities, to monitor other significant environmental developments, and to identify areas of potential interest. These reports, while mostly descriptive and limited in focus, go beyond the raw data and provide analysis of the events in question.

The periodic reports are strategic in nature. They are both descriptive and analytic, require full-scale analysis and synthesis of data, and are broad in scope. They may deal with competitors by outlining competitor strategies, or discuss environmental threats and opportunities in areas of concern to the company. They should be a component of the strategic plan.

How Intelligence Should Be Disseminated to Users

Intelligence can be disseminated by (1) printed reports, (2) verbal communication at meetings, (3) electronic mail, and (4) on-line computer access.

The printed report. The printed report continues to be the mainstay of the business intelligence system and will exist alongside any other dissemination method that may be used.

An acquaintance of ours who had built a thriving business manufacturing and selling paper products for the office was concerned during the early days of the personal computer that he was witnessing the demise of the paper industry and his business along with it. Since then his business has grown and thrives on selling paper for the computer and copy machines.

Verbal communication. In an informal business intelligence system a lot of information is passed around orally, during lunch

Table 9–1. Comparison of four generic reports.

	Critical Intelligence	Situation Reports	Periodic Reports	User-Requested Reports
Type	Strategic/ operational	Strategic/ operational	Strategic	Any
Scope	Specific topic, short, descriptive	Descriptive, focused, limited scope	Broad, in-depth, synthesis; Descriptive/ analytic	Broad or focused
Purpose	Quick dissemination of critical intelligence for immediate action	Monitor competitor activities; Monitor other environmental events; Identify potential areas of interest	Outline competitor strategy; Environmental threats and opportunities; Component of strategic plans	Cover new targets; Up-to-date competitor reports; Special requests
Distribution	UIP/BI personnel	UIP/BI personnel	Senior management	User identified at time of request
Frequency	Ad hoc	Periodic	Periodic	As requested
Format	Bulletin, telephone	Concise, brief, highlights	Background, detailed, analytic, recommendation for action	As requested

meetings, office visits, or official meetings. The formal business intelligence system institutionalizes the oral reporting of intelligence through the analysis committee. In that forum more than just data passes hands. The analysis committee meeting provides the instrument for the synthesis of data into intelligence and at the same time disseminates intelligence to all those present. Of course, whatever consensus has been reached regarding the topic at hand, a printed intelligence report should be generated as well.

Electronic mail. An electronic mail system permits messages to be entered and delivered to a list of addressees. A set of user interest profiles (UIPs), which comprise key words describing the specific interest of the system's users, is maintained on the system. These profiles form a basis for the "content addressable" facility for the system. Any new message entering the system that meets the key word established by the user will automatically be put on that user's mail queue. An electronic mail system may also contain a data base of current messages that the user can scan. This feature is especially valuable when the user develops a new interest that is not reflected in his/her UIP.

On-line computers. If your company has established a computerized BI data base, it may be accessible directly. The system should contain, in addition to raw data, any reports that have been written. Notice of the availability of new reports should be mailed to users or programmed into the computer so that as the user logs on, a message indicates the latest available reports.

Examples of Dissemination Systems

One company with extensive overseas operations has a multi-tiered dissemination system. There are daily intelligence reports that relate mainly to trading opportunities; weekly information summary reports that summarize significant competitive events that have taken place during the previous week; and biweekly reports about economic and political developments in the various countries in which the company does business. Twice a year, comprehensive country reports are compiled. They include information about the country's principal exports and imports, external debt and its implications on government policy, trade balance, GNP, key products, the competitive environment, government policy about trade and protection, and overall assessment of the political and business climate.

Another company, a diversified manufacturer of industrial machinery and consumer appliances, compiles comprehensive competitor profiles about ten major competitors. There are also 25 less extensive profiles of more peripheral competitors. These profiles are available in loose-leaf binders and are generated on the BI computer system. The profiles are updated semiannually. All other intelligence reports are ad hoc reports generated at the request of the user. Once a user-requested report is compiled, it is made available on the computer system for other interested users, unless it is specified that the report should have limited distribution.

Final Word

Several recent developments in software promise to advance the capability of storing and analyzing BI, among them an expert program, developed for the use of army intelligence and marketed by a Massachusetts company, that through the use of artificial intelligence techniques can be used to convert loosely structured textual information into structured data base tables that answer specific questions. The program is also capable of disseminating the intelligence automatically according to user interest profiles. The development of such expert programs, together with the recent successful use of standard text-oriented software at the corporate business intelligence units (CBIUs) of several large corporations, suggests that the BI process will become ever more sophisticated with the ability to easily manipulate large amounts of qualitative data.

In a few years, therefore, there will be no question that computers will play a significant role in establishing a business intelligence capability. Like any other function within the modern firm, the business intelligence process will be transformed by computerization. Without a sophisticated computer capability, a business intelligence system will not fulfill its promise as a true competitive resource for the company.

10

Organizational Structure for the BI System

One of the most significant signs that business intelligence is coming of age in corporate America is the widespread organizational efforts to institutionalize the function. The question companies face today is not whether to systematize the intelligence operation, but what the best organizational solution to the system should be. The process of business intelligence requires that we identify the tasks that must be addressed and the sequence in which they must be completed. We have already identified the tasks of business intelligence. They are collection, evaluation, analysis, storage, and dissemination. The question then becomes how to assign responsibilities for executing these tasks. Obviously, the assignment of tasks for carrying out the business intelligence process is intimately related to decisions about the organizational structure for business intelligence.

There are many questions to be answered regarding assignment of tasks and organizational structure. Should collectors of intelligence data also be analysts? Should analysis be carried out by users or by professional analysts? If by analysts, should they serve the whole organization, or be assigned to particular divisions? Should keying, storing, and retrieval of information be done by information specialists in a separate unit, such as a BI unit or the business library, or should every user be responsible for input and retrieval of information? Should all those involved in managing and carrying out the business intelligence task be part of a centralized BI unit? Or should the BI tasks be distributed among line managers? Should there be corporate involvement in BI? Should it be an exclusively corporate staff function? Should it be exclusively divisional? Could the two approaches be combined?

This chapter will discuss these questions and others pertaining to the organizational structuring of the business intelligence function. The approach to forming a business intelligence function may differ from one firm to another, depending on many variables. Yet, experience over the last several years has brought to the fore some sound principles on which to base BI organizational decisions. Companies have experimented with various approaches to BI and certain useful organizational solutions to the BI function have emerged. These will be discussed in this chapter.

The Five Generic Organizational Structures for BI

Departmental BI.   Under this organizational structure, business intelligence is a fragmented function, carried out within several different functional departments of the organization and serving the needs of the department only. Thus, market research will conduct market studies for the sales and marketing department, and the R&D department will track technological developments for its own needs and purposes. A staff unit responsible for economic analysis will mainly serve the needs of top management, while within the international division, a group of analysts will engage in country risk analysis. The section in charge of corporate development will do analyses of industries and merger candidates. This method of conducting business intelligence—still the prevailing approach—is slowly giving way to more formalized and structured ways of performing the activity.

Decentralized business intelligence.   In a decentralized system, each business unit, subsidiary, or division is in charge of its own business intelligence operations. One person within the business unit is responsible for managing all aspects of the business intelligence function. If the business is small and its information needs modest, that person may perform all the BI functions singlehandedly, from data collection (through the network) to conducting the intelligence analysis and producing intelligence reports. If the business unit is larger, it may have a BI unit consisting of several people, including several analysts each assigned to a different analysis task. A variant of the decentralized system is the strategic business group approach. In this approach several related business units, related in their markets, products, or operations, share a common business intelligence system operated on the group level.

Centralized business intelligence (on the corporate level). In a centralized system there is one business intelligence unit that serves the total organization. The unit manages the collection of data, performs evaluation and analysis, disseminates intelligence reports to all interested users within the organization, and maintains a centralized storage and retrieval system.

The support approach. As in the decentralized system, business intelligence is decentralized and each business unit provides its own intelligence information. This structure differs from the decentralized system in that there also exists a corporate business intelligence unit. Its function is mainly to serve in an educational and advisory role to the business units to help them set up their own business intelligence operations. It may also engage in actual business intelligence work, supplying intelligence relevant to corporate targets that may differ from the needs of any particular business unit. For example, if acquisitions are done on the corporate level, the corporate business unit will provide business intelligence to support the acquisition process.

The complex BI structure. This structure includes a combination of BI activities conducted on the business unit level and on the corporate level. The corporate business intelligence unit typically serves the whole organization and provides business units with intelligence that is common to all of them. At the same time, business units will have business intelligence functions that concentrate on their own unique needs. The corporate BI unit also coordinates the total organizational BI process. In this capacity, its tasks are similar to the tasks of the BI unit in the support approach. In addition, it coordinates the sharing of intelligence generated by business units and functional departments.

The particular structure chosen for the business intelligence process depends on several factors, among them the decisions that business intelligence is to support, the available resources for the BI task on the corporate and business unit levels, the organizational structure of the company, and the prevailing organizational culture. Thus, in organizing the BI system, the particular solution for the firm depends upon its unique circumstances.

The following groups of questions can be of assistance in identifying the relevant factors and in arriving at a decision regarding the appropriate structure of the company's BI system:

1. What kinds of planning and decisions are to be supported with intelligence information? Many kinds of planning are carried on within the various functional areas of the firm and on different levels of the organization. There are operating plans, marketing plans, financial plans, diversification plans, strategic plans, and development plans. The operation of the BI function should be appropriate to the specific needs at the operating levels and at the strategic level and should provide information to support decision making in these areas.

2. What resources relevant to business intelligence does the organization have and where are they located? Are they shared by several business units? These resources include: (a) sources of intelligence data, such as libraries, on-line data bases, and experts within the company; (b) collection network personnel, such as R&D personnel, salespeople, and purchasing agents; (c) intelligence analysts, or employees who could become intelligence analysts on either a full-time or part-time basis; (d) an organization that already manages external data collection and analysis in such areas as market research, economic research, country risk analysis, and planning.

3. How are business units, subsidiaries, or divisions related to each other? Do they deal with the same markets, industries, competitors, clients, or technologies? Do they have similar needs for information? Are they located in one geographical location or in many locations? Do they share any resources such as corporate services, computer systems, production, sales, research, engineering, or service? Does the company do business internationally as well as domestically?

4. What is the corporate structure of the firm? Is it centralized or decentralized? How is strategic planning performed? Is it centralized on the corporate level? Is it completely decentralized and carried out

by line management? Who is responsible for compiling the input that goes into the strategic plans?

These questions can guide those who set out to organize the BI function. They will help answer the questions: Where in the organization should the BI function be located? Should it be established as a corporate BI unit to serve the whole organization, or should each division or business unit be responsible for the creation of its own, separate business intelligence unit? Or is the organization so complex that a combined structure is appropriate? Figure 10–1 is a questionnaire that helps you determine whether a centralized, decentralized, or combined BI organizational structure is best for your organization.

How to Decide on the Appropriate Organizational Structure

This section describes in detail the five organizational structures and provides examples of how a few companies have set up their systems. This should be of assistance in using the questionnaire in Figure 10–1 to decide on an appropriate structure.

The Choice Between Centralized and Decentralized Systems

Figures 10–2 and 10–3 represent the two opposite poles on the continuum of business intelligence organization: the centralized and decentralized business intelligence systems.

A centralized BI system (Figure 10–2) consists of a corporate business intelligence unit (CBIU) that is directly involved in the collection of data from published sources and manages the process of collecting field information. It also performs analysis, and is responsible for storage and dissemination of intelligence. Intelligence targets are determined by the CBIU using input from the total organization. All business intelligence data flow through the corporate group.

In a decentralized system (Figure 10–3), each business unit or division is responsible for its own business intelligence function. Targets and priorities are determined by the division alone and only

Figure 10–1. Questionnaire for establishing a centralized or decentralized system.

---

1. What decisions is the BI system to support?

   Strategic
   Marketing
   Product line
   Diversification
   Acquisitions
   Operating

   Where in the organization do they take place?

2. Is strategic planning currently centralized or decentralized?

3. What is the function of the corporate planning department?

4. Do some or all business units face the same concerns?

   The same markets
   The same competitors
   The same industries
   The same clients
   The same technologies

5. What business units have shared resources?

   Sales force
   Service organization
   R&D
   Engineering
   Manufacturing
   Purchasing
   Market research
   Computer systems
   Electronic mail system
   Business libraries
   Other _____

Figure 10.1   Continued.

6. Do business units have the required resources to establish and operate a BI system?

> Published sources of data
> Field sources of data
> Potential collectors of intelligence
> Computer system and expertise
> A budget for an intelligence system
> Someone to perform intelligence analysis
> Access to outside research
> Someone to coordinate the BI effort

7. Are departments or individuals within the organization currently engaged in analysis tasks?

> Market research
> Economic analysis
> Political analysis
> Issues analysis
> Country risk analysis
> Competitor analysis
> Industry analysis
> Technology analysis

8. List some advantages of centralizing business intelligence on the corporate level in your company.

> a.
> b.
> c.
> d.

9. List some disadvantages of centralizing business intelligence on the corporate level in your company.

> a.
> b.
> c.
> d.

Figure 10.1 Continued.

---

10. List some advantages of creating a separate business
    intelligence process within each business unit/division
    in your organization.

      a.
      b.
      c.
      d.

11. List some disadvantages of creating a separate business
    intelligence process within each business unit/division
    in your organization.

      a.
      b.
      c.
      d.

---

some final intelligence output—intelligence relevant to corporate interests—goes to the staff planning group and to management at the corporate level. In a decentralized system, business units rarely share information with each other.

What type of company will benefit from a centralized business intelligence unit? Obviously, to a single product, single division company, the solution to the question of where to locate the BI function is quite simple and the BI organization is usually housed within either the planning, business development, marketing, or market research departments, or exists as a separate function reporting to the company's chief executive.

At one leading biotechnology company, the business intelligence function was established as a separate information resource center, closely connected with the business library. Two people within the library spend most of their time scanning publications for information to be put on a computerized intelligence data base that serves everyone in the organization. The information resource center is also responsible for maintaining the system information, both field and published, collected by anyone within the organization about numerous large and small biotechnology companies. Users who need information call the librarians with the particular questions they have. Those within the marketing department have direct access into the

Figure 10–2. A centralized BI system.

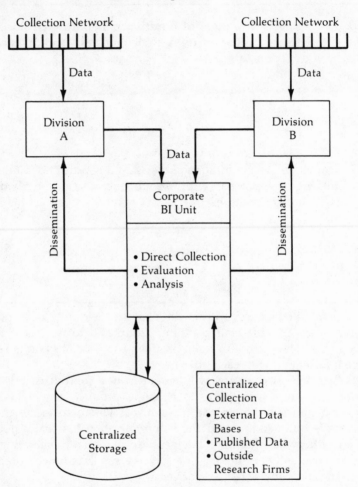

system and do their own research and analysis. The field of biotechnology is diverse and various groups within the company are responsible for different areas that fall under their purview. Yet the central business intelligence unit, with its computerized data base, serves everyone successfully because of the similarity in information structure, sources, and information requirements of the different groups.

Figure 10–3. A decentralized BI system.

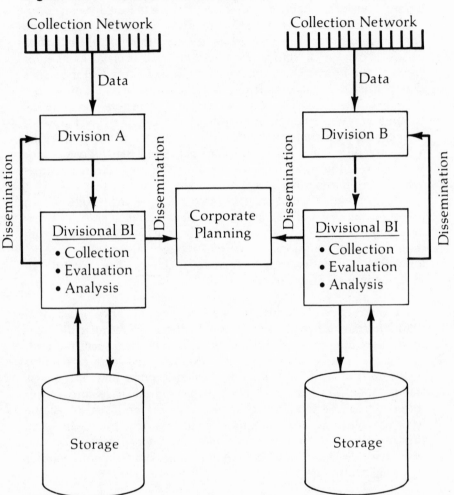

To a multinational or multidivisional corporation with numerous business units in geographically diverse locations, the question of whether to centralize or decentralize BI activities is a critical one. The issue is important because such a company, in attempting to create a central business intelligence unit to serve the whole corporation, may encounter a variety of problems and obstacles. Among them are the following:

Divergent needs.   The analysis produced by corporate analysts in a central business intelligence unit that is shared by all divisions may, in fact, be considered irrelevant by the divisions. A case in point is a large manufacturer that required its divisions to report their BI data to the corporate BI staff and also to compile skeletal competitor reports. The BI staff then put together a book of competitor profiles that consisted of a compilation of reports received from all the divisions. The typical response of division managers was that the competitor profiles did not supply the information they needed, since they contained the information in abbreviated form. It did not make a bit of a difference that the BI staff explained that its competitor profiles were the result of a synthesis of data from various sources within the different divisions.

A corporate BI unit may be able to serve the needs of top managers because of its ability to gain the larger view of the competitive environment. Yet, at the same time, it may have difficulty serving the needs of the divisions, which may require, beyond the strategic, long-term information, much more detail about shorter-term developments in their marketplaces.

Standardization.   A related problem is the tendency of a central BI unit to standardize the intelligence. For firms operating in different industries, different markets, and different countries, such standardization may not be appropriate. For example, the requirements for intelligence of a division in consumer electronics may encompass information about new technologies, new product features introduced by competitors, and changes in styling and design. At the same time, the information required by the subsidiary in the financial markets may need to focus on changes in national income, fluctuations in interest rates, and changes in the regulatory environment for financial institutions.

Industry familiarity.   Collection, and even more so, evaluation and analysis require knowledge of what information is relevant and what is not. Analysis also requires the ability to understand the significance of data. This is especially true for critical field intelligence, the kind brought by salespeople, R&D personnel attending conferences, purchasing agents, and others. The expertise of a centrally located staff group may be limited in scope if they are to track the numerous competitors of a corporation that is a conglomerate of many unrelated businesses. Furthermore, analysts on the corporate level may lack expertise in technical areas as well as intimate knowl-edge of the industries of which they are to keep track. They may be too far removed from the operating units to be able to develop close contacts with experts within the divisions that could aid them in their analysis. This is especially true if the analysts are young MBAs who are very well versed in the latest competitive analysis theories but not as knowledgeable about the day-to-day realities of the industries and competitors they follow.

Too many targets. Even if the central BI unit staff attempts to follow only current competitors, it may compile a list of dozens of companies competing with the various subsidiaries and divisions of a large diversified company. We once saw a list of competitors by product line, compiled by a large pharmaceutical concern, that could have kept an entire CIA unit busy for a year. It is simply impossible for one central BI unit to do a thorough job of tracking the total number of competitors facing a large concern.

Managing the ICN. Some elements of the intelligence process do not easily lend themselves to centralization. Managing the internal collection network from a centralized BI unit can become unwieldy and, as a result, will yield very little information. It is thus not surprising that corporate business intelligence units rely on commer-cial on-line data bases, a business library, trade magazines, newspa-pers and business publications, and firms that provide information-gathering services. To a lesser extent they can rely on personal contacts within the organization to obtain field information. A cor-porate BI program that plans to include field information in its list of sources of intelligence must go beyond the corporate group and build up an intelligence infrastructure in the divisions to manage the collection and communication of field intelligence.

No political base. A subtle problem that we perceive after talking to numerous corporate executives who were put in charge of estab-lishing a BI program is that if the BI unit is centralized, it becomes too people-dependent. Thus, if the individual who is the moving force behind the BI effort leaves, the entire program more often than not will collapse for lack of support. A decentralized BI system seems to offer the executive in charge of the CBIU a political base of support and a cadre of possible heirs. In addition, the simultaneous BI effort shared by several divisions develops opportunities for promotion and an atmosphere of alliance and professional pride among all the people managing the process. This is especially important to the morale of the corporate BI staff who must deal with business unit personnel who often are reluctant to divulge more than they absolutely have to.

Although a completely centralized BI function has its drawbacks, it has advantages as well. First, a centralized BI system offers a strategic corporate overview that enables it to respond quickly to the needs of top management. Second, if the corporation consists of divisions that face similar competitors or operate in similar markets, the unit may be able to serve all the divisions more than adequately. In such a case there is even an advantage to a central unit, since staff analysts will benefit from the wealth of information converging from numerous sources within the various divisions. It thus becomes easier to fill in the gaps in the competitive puzzle. If the company is a diversified firm with businesses competing in unrelated industries, such convergence may not be necessary and may only flood corporate BI staff with impossible amounts of data. Naturally, when the unit serves divisions with similar information needs, duplication in the firm's business intelligence efforts is reduced because BI resources and intelligence information are shared among the various business units. For example, a specialized computerized BI storage system, containing competitor profiles accessible on-line, can be developed to be shared by all business units.

An electronics manufacturer with sales of over five billion dollars has set up a central business intelligence unit (BIU) to serve its various divisions. Its divisions face different markets, but many of the competitors they encounter are common to all of them. The divisions are also concerned with similar technologies. The BIU disseminates information about the general business environment, domestic and international events, competitors, and other related areas, such as technological developments, that are critical to market awareness and competitive success. A special goal is to provide good input to the strategic planning process because management realized there was a need for more informed strategic planning. At the same time, the group's mandate is to support the information needs of operational planning and marketing staffs. The BIU consists of five people. Because of this limitation in resources, intelligence information gathering is limited to published sources only and no field information is used. The sources on which they rely are: newspapers, books, trade magazines, industry studies, government documents, on-line data services, consulting reports, external technology assessment reports, and purchased competitor reports. The limitation of this particular system is its restriction to the use of published sources only. This limitation, however, is not inherent to centralized systems; it is certainly possible for collection of field information to be controlled centrally. In this case, the unavailability of resources and the lack of company-wide commitment to establishing a collection network are the limiting factors. The lack of field information may be particularly damaging to the effort to furnish data for operational planning and to the marketing staff. The marketing department therefore uses field information generated locally and informally in conjunction with the more formal, strategic information they receive from the business intelligence group.

A similar system has been established by a large appliance manufacturer. Although the system also consists of a centralized business intelligence unit that serves the whole organization, it is different from the previous example in that it is much more complex and the business intelligence effort spans the whole organization. One substantial difference is that in addition to using published sources of information, the central unit controls directly a far-flung internal collection network.

There is also a strong commitment by top management to the business intelligence process. This is reflected in the fact that the centrally located business analysis group reports to a manager only one level below the chief executive officer. It thus has high visibility, the endorsement of top management, and the cooperation of the whole organization. Also, by virtue of its direct reporting to top management, it has a direct link to an important group of intelligence users. But the unit does not only serve top management. It is truly a central clearinghouse of competitive information for the whole company.

As regards the collection process, the unit has the dual role of (1) scanning publications and preparing the extracted data for storage, and (2) managing the collection network. The group reads dozens of trade and industry magazines and local newspapers and what is of interest is abstracted and put onto a computerized data base. This process is divided among two groups within the BI unit. One group, which consists of most of the staff within the department, reads the magazines and marks up what is of interest. Three professional abstracters have the full-time job of abstracting those items, using the markings provided by the scanners. While the department covers materials that may be also available on external commercial on-line data bases, it does not necessarily read everything that could be valuable, especially as regards more technical magazines. For this a network within the organization is enlisted on an informal basis. For example, an engineer working on advanced product design may mark up an article dealing with a competitor's use of advanced materials in its new product line. This may be information that has appeared in a technical magazine that the unit does not cover. The unit also manages the collection of field information, and many employees within the company participate. For example, sales and service representatives from all over the country gather information about competitive products and relay it directly to the unit, either over the telephone or through written reports.

The unit, on its part, tries to encourage collectors in order to expand continually the coverage of the network. Any means of communication is accepted to get the information in. Through informal meetings and discussion, unit staff try to get everyone to think of what they can contribute to the strategic data base. Guidelines of what is of interest to the intelligence system are issued regularly. There is, however, no formal method of educating potential collectors on what might be of interest and often collectors send information based on intuition. Although the system lacks a certain needed formality in educating its collection network, it is doing a splendid job in promoting and encouraging the whole concept of business intelligence. Motivation is enhanced by the direct involvement of top management. On a weekly basis a report with the names of people who contributed information that week is sent to top management. The outstanding contributors are singled out. As happens with most collection networks, most of the information tends to come from a small percentage of regular contributors. The group tries to actively encourage people to collect information. Thus, a list of major trade shows is kept, and whenever it is learned that a group of managers and employees is going to a major trade show, the individuals are briefed and encouraged to collect as much information as they can for the intelligence system.

Intelligence data are available to all users directly from the on-line intelligence data base. The unit, besides managing the collection process, provides intelligence reports, such as competitor profiles and industry studies, that are available to whoever is interested. Specific reports are generated on demand. The unit also supports acquisitions. However, such intelligence requests usually deal with industries on which no information is systematically collected, so there often is a need to make use of outside research services.

For many organizations, a centralized business intelligence system is not appropriate. This is true of large companies that consist of several divisions that operate in industries distinct from each other and are organizationally separate and autonomous. A decentralized BI structure is appropriate for such companies, although it may pose certain problems. These are some of the more frequently encountered ones:

Limited perspective.   The concerns of the division are often different from the portfolio considerations of the corporate parent. A business intelligence unit that serves the needs of the division in a decentralized system may not afford the strategic point of view necessary for the corporate parent. Therefore the intelligence needs of the corporation as a whole may not be met by a completely decentralized BI.

Lack of resources.   Often divisions, especially if they are small, do not have the resources, the expertise, and the staff needed to run the BI activity in a formal manner. Also, the participation of employees— other than those on the BI staff itself—is difficult to secure. One typical response from a divisional president was: "My people are already working 11 hours a day. How can I ask them to devote more time to intelligence activities?" Of course, the division president still wanted a full-blown BI program to counter the competitive pressures on his division—that is why his people were working 11 hours a day—but he wanted corporate headquarters to provide the business intelligence services. One resource that divisions may find difficult to take advantage of, though it is coming into prominence as an essential tool in business intelligence, is the sophisticated computer system for the creation of a business intelligence data base. Computerizing the BI function requires investment not only in costly software, but the support system that goes with it. It may not be cost effective for each division to purchase the software, create, and maintain a separate competitive data base. Perhaps, as the computer emerges as an indispensable tool for business intelligence, we may see many more BI systems that are centralized, if not on the overall corporate level, at least by clusters of related business units.

Waste. There may be a duplication of effort between several divisions, especially if they operate in the same or similar industries, face similar markets, or compete with the same companies. Despite the existence of such unifying factors, many companies have found it impossible to create a common business intelligence system. The reason is that independent business units within a corporation, especially those that compete with each other, do not as a rule exchange intelligence.

An interesting example of a decentralized system that ran into such problems is that of an industrial corporation that manufactures components used in heavy machinery. The company has two divisions: One manufactures the product and sells it to OEMs; the other only markets the product and sells it as a replacement part to the aftermarket. The latter division has higher margins and provides the lion's share of profits for the company. Traditionally there has been rivalry between the two divisions, so that little information is exchanged between them. Each division has conducted its own business intelligence operations separately, despite the fact that they sell the same product and face almost the same cluster of competitors. Each has a complete file system about competitors and a person responsible for maintaining the files and creating competitive profiles that are practically identical. Each division of course deals with matters relating to its own limited area of concern, that is, competition relating to the OEM market in the one division, and competition relating to the aftermarket in the other. Neither provides a complete strategic picture encompassing both markets. In fact, the problems manifested by the dichotomous BI system reflect a deeper schism. The company's R&D, as well as production operations, belong to the OEM division, and research has gone in the direction of producing a component that will need no replacement. Such a component, when it is finally brought to market, will undermine the more profitable division of the company. Yet the company continues with business as usual, not only perpetuating the dichotomous BI system that gives the corporate parent a partial picture at best, but, more critically, perpetuating a dichotomous strategic direction that may harm its own long-term profitability.

Under the appropriate circumstances, there can be distinct advantages to a decentralized system. First, if the division has its own business intelligence operations, business intelligence questions and needs can be answered faster and there may be fewer conflicts over priorities in answering these needs. Then, too, analysts become knowledgeable about the industry, product lines, and competitors of the particular division. They can be in close contact with experts within the division in such areas as R&D, production, marketing, and service. Another advantage is that BI personnel are closer to the collection network and can more easily control and direct the flow of incoming data. Because the division only deals with intelligence data relating to its own industry, the amount of data with which analysts have to deal is manageable.

We would like to caution the reader about one pitfall in establishing a BI system. You may end up with a decentralized system, although the stated objective may be to structure a centralized system. Whether a system is centralized or decentralized depends upon where the critical tasks of the intelligence process are performed and not on the label attached to a particular organizational function. An example will clarify the issue and its importance: A company in the communications industry decided to set up a centralized business intelligence function to be run by corporate staff. The intelligence unit was to serve the needs of all divisions, large and small, many of which operated in similar markets. The corporate unit consisted of two staff members. Their function was not to collect data or conduct analysis but to compile competitor profiles for some 30 competitors, based on analysis provided by the divisions. Each division was responsible for collecting data on its competitors and putting together initial competitor profiles. These profiles were sent to corporate staff who combined all the profiles from the various divisions into unified competitor profiles, which in turn were made available to all the divisions. Very quickly it became obvious that this method of conducting business intelligence had no advantages. On the contrary, the divisions felt that they were doing all the work but getting nothing in return. To start with, the profiles, by attempting to digest information from all the divisions, were skeletal and did not serve the needs of the divisions, although they were helpful for top management. Second, in assembling the profiles the analysts attempted to reconcile sometimes contradictory information that came from different divisions without consulting the divisions. In doing so, divisions became distrustful of the information and tended to disregard the profiles. Finally, smaller divisions did not have the personnel to compile reports; they had to content themselves with whatever competitor profiles were relevant to their needs.

This BI system is ostensibly a centralized system. But practically all the BI work, from collection of data to analysis and creation of competitor profiles, was carried out by the divisions. The system was in fact a decentralized system. The central staff unit added little value to the process of intelligence creation. Rather, it may have caused harm because it alienated the divisions. The major beneficiaries of the intelligence unit were three corporate executives, one of them the manager of the system, who relied on the information contained in the competitor profiles. Once the manager of the system left, the system fell into complete disuse and finally the corporate unit was disbanded.

The Support Approach

A variant of the decentralized system attempts to correct some of its failings by incorporating a central BI function. We call this structure the "support approach." In addition to business intelligence carried out by each individual division, a business intelligence unit limited in size is established at the corporate level. Its main mission is to provide support to the divisional BI functions, where the main BI effort is carried out. The corporate BI unit (CBIU) is responsible for the following tasks:

- Educating managers and employees throughout the corporation about BI
- Serving as quality control to the BI activities at the divisional level
- Offering consulting to divisions in areas of expertise that may not exist within divisions, such as assistance in setting up a computer system
- Conducting BI analysis for corporate targets

The last task is usually secondary to the other missions of the corporate unit and is reserved for those corporate concerns that otherwise fall between the cracks. In this case, the CBIU provides collection, evaluation, and analysis services to corporate management. This task is practical only as long as the number of targets is kept reasonably low, which means that only those targets or critical intelligence needs that are not covered by BUs should be considered for CBIU targeting. Otherwise, the corporate intelligence specialists find themselves engaged in endless ad hoc projects and have time for little else.

The other missions are those typical of a supporting corporate BI function. In its role as educator, the CBIU promotes business intelligence within the entire corporation. Often, if the corporation consists of independent business units, the business units have the final decision whether to invest resources in establishing a business intelligence function and how. It is the function of the CBIU to cajole them into setting up a system in compliance with the ideas generated by the corporate unit. The business units have to be made aware of the significance of the new function to the survival of the corporation. Corporate BI staff use various means to increase business unit management awareness and acceptance of the necessity of a BI function. It may publish a company-wide newsletter demonstrating the results of successful BI programs at various business units; it may set up intelligence awareness briefings, make BI presentations, or send managers to BI seminars; or it may bring together managers from various business units to discuss the establishment of a joint business intelligence program. As part of its educational function, the CBIU may also provide training for BI personnel at the business unit level.

As part of its quality control function, the CBIU continually monitors BI activities to ensure the BI system is appropriately implemented so as to assure the quality of the collected intelligence. Quality control is achieved by setting standards for the entire system. These standards apply to the determination of targets, modes of reporting BI, codes of ethics, description of accountability, and standard procedures for evaluation.

At a large chemical corporation, where the most difficult problem in developing the corporate strategic plan was the lack of corporate trust in the environmental/competitive input provided by the divisions, the standardization and checks on the intelligence activities of the business units was the main goal of the CBIU. The rationale was that if corporate staff could not independently verify the accuracy of the data that went into the business units' strategic plans, it could at least ensure that the procedures used to gather the data were of high quality.

Finally, the CBIU may serve in a consulting role, providing technical advice on the latest BI techniques, and information technology for BI purposes. For example, corporate staff will have knowledge about the latest computerized means for storing, retrieving, and analyzing BI information. It will be able to advise divisions about available software programs appropriate for the business intelligence task and how to implement their use.

The corporate management of a diversified conglomerate with interests in the chemical, automotive, and machinery industries realized that better planning required better information. Their first step to accomplish the goal of better information was to assign a person from the corporate planning department the task of finding out how other companies obtained and used competitive information. Then, within the corporate planning department, a three-person business intelligence unit was established. Management realized, however, that because of the diversity of its business, its geographical dispersion, including overseas business, and the sheer size of the organization, it was impractical to attempt to carry out the business intelligence function on the corporate level. It was decided to encourage the various businesses to establish their own business intelligence systems. The three corporate staff members prepared a program about business intelligence and its implementation that they presented to the management of every business unit. It was up to each business unit to decide whether to establish a BI function and what scope and structure would be appropriate for its own situation. The role of the corporate unit did not end with the initial presentation. The corporate unit was available for consultation as each business unit embarked on the process of establishing a BI function. In addition, a year after the process was launched, management from all the business units was brought together at a three-day retreat where presentations were made by outside experts about methods of development and control of the BI function, and business units reported on the progress of their efforts to incorporate BI into their operations, the successes with which they met, and obstacles they encountered.

The Combined Structure

Some conglomerates consist of completely independent business units. In most companies, however, business units are not totally unrelated. Many businesses share resources, such as manufacturing, distribution, marketing, or R&D. In addition, businesses also share concerns, resulting from mutual clients, similar products and technologies, or overlapping geographical coverage. In such large, diversified, and organizationally complex corporations, the business intelligence system may itself take on a complicated structure, conforming to the complexity of the organization it is to serve to meet the needs of the organization most effectively. The solution for such an organization may be to combine decentralized BI structural elements with a centralized business intelligence function. As the example below will show, such a business intelligence setup may consist of divisional BIUs that cater to their own divisional needs, and a central business unit that caters to corporate needs, provides some business intelligence services common to all the divisions, and serves as a company-wide BI coordinator.

Company K is a diversified manufacturer. Its business units sell to both consumer and industrial markets. Many of its products are technologically related. Thus, while its business units are independent, some of them share manufacturing facilities and rely on a common R&D organization. Related business units are grouped into strategic groups. In addition to its core of traditional businesses, several new businesses—recent acquisitions of small entrepreneurial companies—function as business units, but are quite independent and their links with the rest of the company are weak. The organizational structure of Company K and its BI function is shown in Figure 10-4.

Company K has enjoyed a very strong position in many of its markets. Recent events, however, have steered it away from its traditional, now mature, markets, where it has become progressively more difficult to obtain decent returns on investment. This is the reason for the new acquisitions. The bulk of its sales and earnings still comes from its traditional product lines. Management perceived the need to bolster its competitive position, and the first step was an attempt to better understand its competitive environment and the risks and opportunities that it posed. Corporate management surveyed its existing environmental scanning practices. As a worldwide company with international presence in many countries, the company had an established country risk analysis group. There was also a small group engaged in economic analysis. Otherwise, each business unit conducted its own market research, and informal competitive and industry analyses, mostly on an ad hoc basis.

Management's first step in formalizing business intelligence at Company K was to consolidate the various corporate support groups involved in environmental analysis, including the economic analysis and country risk analysis groups. Next, management realized that many of the information needs of its business units overlapped, because of either common technologies, common competitors, or common markets. It therefore added staff to the newly established

Figure 10-4. Organizational structure of Company K.

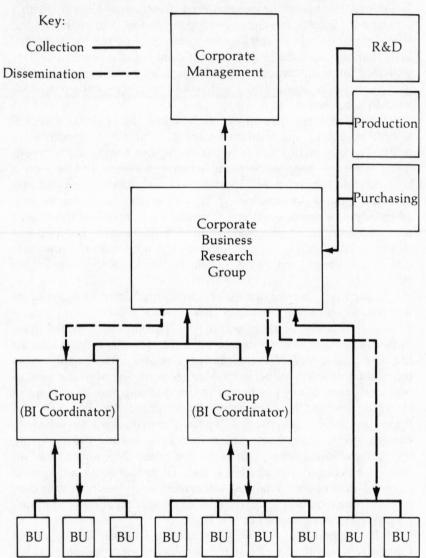

corporate business research group. The task of the new staff members was to scan a list of publications, including technical publications, newspapers, and local papers, for information relevant to the needs common to all the business units. A data base containing all the information was created. Following this start, as the unit increased in size to almost 30 people, it took on the task of conducting research and intelligence analysis for the business units.

Most of the intelligence generated by the corporate research group deals with topics of interest to all the business units, including general industry studies, technology trends that might affect the corporation as a whole, and competitive profiles of the major competitors. Business units have access to the data base of raw data and may request any information that will enable them to conduct their own business intelligence analysis for issues that concern them alone. Thus, each of the larger business units has at least one person in charge of business intelligence. In addition to conducting intelligence analysis, the person serves as coordinator of intelligence between the corporate research unit and the business unit.

A survey conducted by the corporate business research group showed that many informal contacts within the organization yielded valuable intelligence to those who had the contacts. It was found that the R&D group conducted its own informal technology assessment, for its own purposes, and provided some information to those outside the group with whom they had close contact. Similarly, manufacturing had intelligence information about competitors' manufacturing facilities that they collected for their own use. The corporate business research group decided to formalize such information sharing by advertising to the business units the availability of information from other departments, such as R&D and manufacturing, and by channeling requests for information through the corporate group. This has led to a greater awareness within the organization of the value of the corporate business research group. In a slow, informal process, many within the organization have begun to forward information to the business research group. This, the company believes, may be the beginning of a more formal collection network. For now the research group encourages anyone with information to relay it to the group. To facilitate communication, any method of transmission convenient to the collector is used. Collectors may use written communications, the telephone, and the existing electronic voice messaging. Obviously, this new development has raised the question of what role the corporate research group is to play in the business intelligence process. It was initially structured to provide only more global information common to all business units. Now, more and more information, especially field information, that is specific to particular business units is reaching the group. With the recent addition of a computerized data base accessible to all business units, it seems more likely that the unit will serve as a clearinghouse for all types of information. Because of sheer volume of information needs and the demand for knowledge specific to particular business units, most of the intelligence analysis that concerns the business unit is still carried on by the analyst at the business unit level. The latest addition to the business intelligence system is a BI coordinator on the group level who coordinates the sharing of intelligence among business units belonging to its strategic business group.

As the above examples demonstrate, a business intelligence organization can change dramatically between its inception and its mature functioning structure. As with other organizational functions, the organization may evolve as experience is gained and as new needs emerge.

Where the BI Unit Should Be in the Organization

In our discussion so far, we have assumed an independent BIU, whether on the corporate level or within a business unit. Not all business intelligence units, however, are independent, and whether they are separate or part of another department, whether they reside within a particular functional area or report directly to the president, varies greatly from firm to firm. To a certain extent, the diversity of organizational solutions can be traced to the fact that all corporations engage in informal BI activities to one degree or another, and that these activities tend to concentrate in certain functional areas more than in others. A formal BI function is not created in a vacuum. The result is that different companies build their newly organized BI effort around different existing BI centers. For example, marketing departments in many corporations engage in some form of BI operations, especially those related to pricing and product positioning; R&D departments may be actively pursuing technological intelligence; economics departments, where they exist, conduct some type of environmental monitoring and analysis; the new business development departments conduct BI activities to support their scenario-building exercises; and the corporate library may engage in data base searches for everyone. Each of these may serve as a core around which to mold a business intelligence system. Often, the BI system springs up where there is someone to fight for it. Unless there is a conscious decision by top management to weigh the various possibilities for structuring the business intelligence function and then to set it up in a manner most appropriate for its mission, the development of a business intelligence function will be an evolutionary process and the function may end up anywhere within the organization, not necessarily in a place where it can be most effective.

A large pharmaceutical company had an enthusiastic executive for the business intelligence function in the person of a vice president in charge of market development for the company's largest division. Within the marketing department the VP had two groups that were already responsible for some environmental scanning: One provided market research services to the division, and the other studied larger issues, such as the regulatory environment and social attitudes toward the pharmaceutical industry. The VP, with the approval of his boss, the division manager, set up a third unit, which was called the competitive analysis group. The group was to serve not only the needs of the largest division, within which it was located, but also those of the three other smaller divisions. With great enthusiasm two competitive analysts and one information specialist began organizing the group. They made known to everyone they knew within the organization that they were in business. They also initiated meetings with various potential users and potential field sources of information within the company to enlist their cooperation. They realized quickly, however, that acceptance was slow to materialize. When we sat down to analyze the reasons, several things became obvious: Part of the group's problem was the traditional structure. Like market research, which served the division only and marketing specifically, the analysis group was housed within marketing. This did not promote an image of a group devoted to the interests and concerns of the whole organization, including the various divisions and the various levels of management. Also, since the executive who championed the BIU was from marketing, there was little direction from top management itself. As a result, the program suffered from a lack of company-wide promotion. Obviously, when an enthusiastic BI manager has little active support from top management, matters may become politically sensitive. The optimal organizational solution in this case would be to move the group from within the largest division's marketing department and transform it into a corporate function, but it may consequently lose the direct support of its eager VP and thereby lose its momentum.

The fact that informal BI activities and some formal environmental scanning processes are always carried out in the typical corporation suggests that in organizing a formal BI function one should rely as much as possible on existing channels and centers of BI activities. Careful consideration should be given to whether existing structures can serve as part of the formal business intelligence process or whether the function should be built from scratch with a brand-new business intelligence department. Often, careful restructuring can bring together under one roof various groups that have previously functioned separately and have reported to diverse departments. These can serve as the locus for a new, independent business intelligence unit. Thus, such traditional functions as market research, economic analysis, country risk analysis, and industry analysis can form the core of a new BI unit. The advantage of using existing groups and organizational entities is that it usually facilitates the acceptance of change by the organizational bureaucracy.

The BI Committees

Not uncommonly, the success of the BI function rests with the individual who champions it. This is a familiar aspect of any new organizational idea. The ability of that prime mover to promote the idea of business intelligence to win acceptance, exposure, and political backing can be enhanced significantly through the formation of BI committees. Committees can interfere with the decision-making process or they can encourage it and then accelerate implementation. From design to implementation, the use of BI committees is probably the best way to institutionalize the BI function.

There are several possible committees that may be used. The basic principle behind using the committees is the same as that behind the internal collection network: the sharing of responsibility. Accordingly, committees such as an intelligence committee, a users committee, and an analysis committee can be used for the implementation of a collection network, determination of targets, analysis, and so on.

The Intelligence Committee

Perhaps the single most challenging problem for the BI unit is to obtain and maintain the active involvement of line managers and the various functional departments in the acquisition and communication of external information. The intelligence committee oversees the implementation and further development of the BI function. It should include representatives from the various departments and functional areas that are directly involved in the BI activity, for example, sales, marketing, and planning. The committee can be structured either as a temporary team or as a standing intelligence committee. The activities of the committee should be directed by the BIU personnel. Its agenda is determined by the BI unit with input and suggestions from committee participants. At the regular committee meetings, department representatives present progress reports on the implementation of the intelligence activities in their respective departments. Examples of intelligence gathered by the various departments should serve to highlight the problems and achievements in the BI efforts of each department. The intelligence committee helps improve the quality of the output from each collection area by using and sharing the knowledge and experience of the representatives to the committee. It also helps create high visibility and acceptance of business intelligence throughout the company, and thus promote the use of intelligence information in organizational decision-making processes. Experience shows that if line managers do not become involved in the business intelligence process, they either downplay the relevance of intelligence or simply ignore its usefulness.

One of the advantages of an intelligence committee is that it helps tailor the collection network to the modus operandi of each group or department. The representatives of each group are more aware than BI personnel of what would work best with their own group. They can also give immediate feedback about problems encountered in establishing a workable collection system in their department. A representative of a department can both facilitate the implementation of a collection network and at the same time monitor closely progress and participation by the department.

The Users Committee

The main purpose of the users committee is to get the users of intelligence actively involved in the BI process. One of the major functions of the BI unit is to coordinate the BI activities of the various individuals and departments, rather than perform the BI tasks (such as collection) themselves. The BI staff therefore encourages user involvement as a way of getting the organizational support it needs. One BI director recounted how the first response of his organization to the formation of the BIU was skepticism. When the director persisted in pressing managers to use his unit for getting information, a few obliged by asking very basic questions. Once these questions were answered, the users started to demand answers to tougher questions and gave the BI staff more complex assignments. Soon the unit was swamped by requests for information about everything under the sun. The users committee is one way to solicit such a demand for intelligence, demand that eventually improves the quality of decisions made in the firm.

Once the BI function has the attention of its "clients," it must continue to maintain it. One way to ensure user participation is to constantly involve the users in determining its exact course. This need to keep the BI function in continual touch with the various organizational users of BI should figure prominently in the organizational solution for the BI system. It is a sad but familiar finding of organizational scientists that much of the information collected by a typical organization is never actually used. This is where the users committee plays an important role. It serves as a forum where decision makers can share ideas about the use of intelligence and where the BI unit can promote the use of its product. The committee meetings also serve as a tool for soliciting feedback from users about changes in their information needs. (The analysis committee is discussed in the following section.)

Organizing and Managing the Analysis Function

Analysis is the process by which large amounts of data are evaluated and condensed to a form that can feasibly and easily be used in the decision-making process. The format should be directly usable in both the strategic planning process and day-to-day decisions. The purpose of analysis is to make information more compact, condensed, meaningful, and easy to access and absorb. There are several tasks of the analysis process. These tasks may not be completely independent of each other, or necessarily consecutive, but they help us define the nature of analysis. An understanding of the component tasks of the analysis process is important for two reasons. First, the understanding of how intelligence should be derived from data ensures that the ultimate intelligence product is useful and valid. Second, if the analysis function is to be allocated to several staff and/ or line managers, it will be necessary to assign component tasks.

The analysis process consists of six tasks: collating data, condensing information, drawing conclusions, building scenarios, studying implications for competitive positioning, and suggesting recommendations for action. The first step in the analysis process requires that related data be collated. That is, discrete pieces of data should be assembled to provide information building blocks (IBBs). For example, all data regarding the manufacturing facilities of a competitor should be included in one category. This category may contain all the specific detail available about the competitor's manufacturing plants, their number and size, their location, the type of manufacturing equipment used in them, control procedures, the number of employees at each location, availability of transportation, and proximity to raw material suppliers. The next step involves condensing the information because so many bits and pieces of data are difficult to handle separately. Once the information is categorized and condensed conclusions may be drawn. What is the manufacturing capability of the competitor? Are its plant and equipment new and efficient? Is the competition using the latest manufacturing technologies? What does this imply for its manufacturing costs? For the flexibility of its production line? For its ability to switch facilities among product lines? Does it have proprietary process technology that may give it a competitive edge? Is it benefiting from shared production facilities among various strategic business units? Are its transportation costs high because of its geographical location? Does it have exit barriers relating to the manufacturing facilities? Is it suffering from idle capacity?

Following this analysis, it is useful to draw several possible scenarios of competitor actions and responses. This will pave the way to assessing your own company's competitive position. Of course, this stage requires that you possess both information about the competitor and knowledge of your company's strengths and weaknesses. Finally, analysis is followed by recommendations for action resulting from the assessment of competitive positioning.

The separation of the analysis function into its component tasks shows that there is more to competitive analysis than the creation of a profile consisting merely of a laundry list of the competitor's assets. Unfortunately, this is all too often what you find: analysis that consists of a long list of the competitor's facilities, its product line, a description of its sales and service policies, its sales force, its management background, and so on, with very little beyond that. This is only the first stage of analysis. What makes the result true intelligence is the further processing of the information.

As noted above, the analysis task is in fact a group of tasks, each of which requires an increasing degree of skill and knowledge. Who, then, should do the analysis? Should one person be responsible for the complete task of analysis, from data collation to analysis and recommendations for action? If so, who should that person be? Are there other ways of performing intelligence analysis? Should the components of the analysis function be allocated among several people? If so, whom?

There are several alternative ways for organizing the analysis function.

Alternatives for the Analysis Function

Centralized/decentralized
  Analysis is a corporate function
  Analysis is a divisional function
  Combined structure: some analysis is corporate and some
    divisional
Distributed analysis
  Person in charge of strategic planning
  Analyst or analysis group
  Analyst with input from experts in the organization
  Analysis distributed among users
  Analysis committee

Centralized or Decentralized Analysis

Whether the analysis function is to be centralized or decentralized depends on the general structure for the BI system. As we have seen in previous examples, the analysis function may be part of the corporate business intelligence unit, where analysis is performed by staff analysts. Alternatively, analysis may be performed within each business unit. The analysis function may also be divided between a corporate business intelligence unit and the local business unit, with each allocated different areas of analysis. Even within these three types of structures—the centralized, the decentralized, and the combined—there can be considerable variations. For example, at one large multinational corporation, there is not one but two corporate business intelligence units. One unit, a corporate staff function, monitors economic, social, cultural, and political development, and broad trends in industry. It draws strictly on published sources. The other unit, which is also a corporate staff unit, specializes in industry/competitive/market analysis. It relies on published sources, such as trade publications, newspapers, and government sources, as well as field sources of information provided by the whole organization.

At another large corporation there are also two corporate business intelligence functions. Again, one is an intelligence unit that is made up of a group of experts who do economic analysis, political analysis, and broad issues analysis. This unit mostly serves top management. The other corporate intelligence function is affiliated with the corporate library, and is responsible for circulating to everyone within the organization information such as articles from business, trade, and technical magazines.

Distributed Analysis

The analysis function, following the grand structure of the business intelligence system, may be centralized, decentralized, or combined. The question remains, however, of who will do the analysis. The options for allocating the analysis task range from one person performing the task, to a whole group of staff analysts, to the broad-based participation of many employees. Some alternatives in performing intelligence analysis are outlined below.

Person in charge of strategic planning. Throughout the book we have referred to the business intelligence unit, one of the functions of which is to conduct analysis. Not all companies have a business intelligence unit. They may be too small to have a unit devoted to the task. This may also be the case with a small division within a large corporation. In such instances a logical candidate for the intelligence analysis task is the person who performs strategic planning. Strategic planning done in a vacuum is useless. Every strategy needs to take into account the external and competitive environment. The person performing strategic planning thus is a major consumer of competitive information and is the logical person to generate competitive intelligence. If the additional task of intelligence analysis proves to pose high demands on the person's time, the person may be assisted by someone else within the organization. As mentioned previously, the analysis task is actually a combination of several tasks. Thus, someone may be assigned to do the initial, time-consuming step in the analysis—the collating and condensing of data—leaving the part that requires drawing conclusions, building scenarios, and recommending action to the strategic planner.

Analyst or analysis group. In a larger setting analysis will be performed by a professional staff analyst or a group of analysts. An advantage of analysis performed by staff analysts who are not involved in the day-to-day operation of the business is that they have a degree of objectivity. Staff analysts also may be able to bring wider knowledge and experience in diverse industries to the analysis task. In addition, staff analysts may be specially trained in conducting analysis. There may also be disadvantages to using staff analysts. If they have little line experience and no real intimate knowledge of the industries they analyze, they may lack a practical feel for the business and their analyses may be too academic. They may also be removed from the concerns of decision-makers. However, that can be alleviated by structuring the BI process in such a way that there is close contact between decision-makers and analysis group staff members. One way to promote close contact is through the users committee discussed earlier in this chapter. A typically encountered problem, and not only in the area of competitive analysis, is that staff may lack credibility with line managers. As a result, the reports they generate are not used. Again, such a problem can be alleviated if the reports are geared to answer specific needs of decision-makers.

The dangers of isolating a staff analysis function from the concerns and needs of the organization can be demonstrated with the following example. One of our clients built up an impressive business intelligence system. It decided to generate two kinds of competitive profiles. The first consisted of a one-page profile of some 50 different competitors. The other competitive profile was to be a comprehensive report on only 7 competitors. The initial effort concentrated on producing the 50 short profiles and soon these were disseminated among decision-makers. The response, however, was not positive. The consensus was that the profiles were quite useless. They were too short for those who needed competitive information and contained little that was unknown; for those who were not interested in the competitors at all, the information was irrelevant.

A reverse problem that one encounters with staff reports is analysis that leaves nothing out. This situation can arise if analysts do not know how reports are going to be used or are not given the authority to make the determination of which information is crucial (and therefore should be included) and which information can be omitted. This problem is easy to control. First, analysts should have a good understanding of their own company, its organizational structure, and the function of the various decision-makers who are their clients. Whether through the intelligence audit, through the users committee meetings, or by other, perhaps more informal means, they should understand what the reports they generate are used for. Then, whenever staff analysts are asked to provide custom-made reports, they should query the user as to the specific use of the report. Often, this initial interactive process serves not only to educate the analyst, but to clarify to the person requesting the report what information is actually needed. This will save time and effort spent on information irrelevant to the decisions the report is to support, and may lead to the inclusion of more pertinent information.

For example, the management of a pharmaceutical company requested from its staff BI unit an urgent report on a competitor and its plans to bring to market a new drug. Typically, it takes at least five years for a new drug to be approved by the FDA, and sometimes much longer. The competitor was in the early stages of the process, but management felt that to meet the threat adequately they needed information early on, especially about the possible formulation of the drug and how it was to be positioned in the market. The information they asked the analyst to provide included everything from what was known about the drug, its uses and formulations, to the competitor's availability of manufacturing facilities. In a preliminary discussion with management, the analyst pointed out that at this point knowledge of the competitor's exact manufacturing capabilities was irrelevant to their capability to bring to market the drug. In the time span of five or more years to drug approval, the competitor would be able to construct new manufacturing facilities, so current facilities were not indicative of future capabilities. Then, of course, manufacturing of the drug might be done by subcontractors, and such arrangements would not be apparent until much later. Thus, effort was conserved by clarifying the actual useful information for the decision-maker, and this helped the analyst to concentrate the critical intelligence needs.

Analyst with input from experts in the organization. This set-up is a variant of the previous structure and because of its effectiveness, should be encouraged as much as possible. When analysts in the staff function have no line experience, technical knowledge, and so forth, they should rely on a network of experts within the company. It is important, however, to make use of a network of experts anyway because analysts are unlikely to have the range of expertise of a whole group of experts.

A defense manufacturer, in the following example, was able to creatively use the concept of a network of experts to augment the competitive analysis performed by its two staff competitor analysts. The method was designed to both tap into the knowledge of the experts, and, at the same time, to avoid their biases and opinions created through years of competition with the same group of companies. The way information was obtained from experts was as follows: If input on the financial status of the competitors was needed, financial statements of the particular competitor were given to the finance department, with all identifying information blackened out. The department then provides a complete financial analysis of the statements without knowledge of who the actual company was. Similarly, information about manufacturing equipment and facilities of the competitor was given to the manufacturing people without identifying the company. Based on the information provided, they assessed the technical capability of the competitor and its capability to effectively compete in the bidding process of particular programs. Similarly, if it were known that the competitor was purchasing parts from a particular supplier or was dealing with a particular subcontractor, the purchasing department was asked to comment on the implication of the fact on the competitor's product quality, price, and delivery terms.

Analysis distributed among users. Managers often perform intelligence analysis for their own needs. This usually happens by necessity, when there is no budget to hire staff analysts or there is no one else who can take on the task of doing analysis for all users in the organization. Analysis performed by managers may also happen by design. There are two advantages to managers doing competitive analysis.

First, it is likely that if managers perform competitive analysis, they will see it as an integral part of the planning process and will integrate the intelligence into their strategic decisions. Another advantage of involving middle managers in the competitive analysis process is that it is a method to train them to think strategically, a trait that is a necessary part of becoming a successful general manager.

A problem of allocating competitive analysis among managers is that the intelligence function loses one of the important features brought about by the formal business intelligence system: the centralization of intelligence collection and analysis, to take advantage of all information within the organization. This disadvantage of user-generated analysis can be mitigated by the existence of a staff business intelligence unit that does part of the analysis work, including collating, condensing, and drawing some conclusions. The rest of the task is left to the manager, including building scenarios, analyzing of competitive positioning, and drawing implications for strategy and action by the company.

Analysis committee. A last method of conducting analysis involves the analysis committee. It is not advisable to conduct intelligence analysis through a committee only, since the process can be time-consuming and require elaborate coordination. It therefore should be reserved only for major assessments of the competition and competitive positioning.

The analysis committee is loosely composed of managers from various functional and product groups in the company. Members of the group should work together, either as a permanent analysis committee or in a role-playing, ad hoc committee, to provide a composite competitor profile to assess the competitive standing of the company.

There are several benefits to the analysis committee. The expertise of its participants is brought to bear on the information at hand, and the various perspectives provide a richer analytic and intuitive evaluation of intelligence with respect to the competitive positioning of the company. This enables the group to approach the intelligence data in a way unavailable to the individual analyst. The interactive process of the analysis group enables participants to develop new perceptions and change existing ones. And since the participants are simultaneously the end-users as well as the analyzers of the intelligence, their involvement in the BI program is of major importance.

During analysis sessions, intelligence needs are crystallized, targets and priorities emerge much more clearly, and benefits accruing from the system become more apparent. Also, the committee form ensures that competitive analysis assessments reflect as little manager bias as possible and that a broad view of the competition is gained. This decreases the danger that managers may reach conclusions tainted by rigid opinions created over many years of dealing with the same competitors. Because personal bias and individual parochial viewpoints can taint the analysis, it is desirable that committee participants have some conceptual framework that will facilitate the analysis and will direct their thinking into more future-oriented directions. This is yet another reason why managers should be trained in competitor analysis (see the chapter on CINs).

It should be kept firmly in mind that in a committee, the analysis that emerges is the result of a negotiation process. Inherent in such a process are several risks. The analysis may provide too conservative a profile of the competitor, since a common denominator among the various members has to be found. As opposed to staff analysts who have no vested interests, the group—consisting of managers with a stake in the outcome—may block out information negative to their own company; the result may be a distorted competitive picture. Indeed, a consensus may emerge where none is possible and conflicting pieces of information may be reconciled just to end a meeting with a tidy piece of analysis.

There is another benefit to the analysis committee that is important for the emerging business intelligence system. Through the analysis committee, the ability of the BIU to serve the decision-making needs of the various users, as well as to receive political support for its operation, can be markedly enhanced. Beyond improving the analysis, the group has a significant role in promoting the effectiveness of the BI system. During the analysis sessions, gaps in intelligence are identified, targets and priorities are updated, potential sources of intelligence may be suggested, and, most important, the benefits of a formal BI system are demonstrated in practice. It is one thing to try and convince potential users and collectors with the help of a theoretical argument that they will benefit from a well-organized intelligence effort; it is quite another to involve them in an analysis committee where participants get firsthand experience in the issues concerning intelligence.

The business unit serves as the coordinating body for the analysis committee. As part of this responsibility, it prepares the input to these meetings. Any available data that could be of use to committee members in their periodic analyses should be collated, condensed, and prepared by the BIU staff. BIU personnel also maintain the administrative details of the meetings and are responsible for the compilation of the final analysis that emerges from the sessions, including the distribution of results.

Implementing and Managing the BI System

The business intelligence system that we advocate in this book calls for the inclusion and participation of all levels of the organization and all employees. This is why implementing the BI system to carry out the BI process can be accomplished neither quickly, nor in one step.

How to Implement the BI System

In implementing a BI system, two kinds of control have to be established. The first involves the use of rules, procedures, and organizational structure to guide the behavior of participants. The other involves a much more subtle form of control, specifically the influencing of behavior through shaping the norms, values, and beliefs of managers and employees. The use of organizational structures and rules is the less complicated aspect of implementation and may be accomplished speedily, once a decision has been made about the specific structures for BI.

For the BI system to succeed, everyone should be enlisted in the BI process. Collectors should participate in the collection network; decision-makers should learn to use the system and its intelligence output to support their decisions. Participation of everyone within the organization requires that a positive company-wide attitude be adopted.

This can be accomplished by several means:

Using demonstrations rather than words to communicate the desired new activities.   One way of doing this is to introduce change first in one division and demonstrate the success of the system there, before trying to sell the rest of the organization on the idea of business intelligence. The division where the initial process is to be implemented should be chosen carefully. It should be a division where any of the following conditions exist: (1) The division has already in place some of the components of business intelligence that can successfully be incorporated into a BI system; (2) the organizational culture is such that everyone is already very attuned to the competitive environment; (3) the division has a great need for intelligence but currently does not have the needed intelligence, so any improvement in the acquisition and analysis of information will prove a great success and will demonstrate the value of formal BI.

Focusing early efforts on the needs that are already recognized as important. The BI function has to prove its value. It is therefore essential to show early success, even though the program itself is at its inception. There is nothing like success to draw the support of the organization. The best place to show success is where it would count most.

Having solutions presented by persons who have high credibility in the organization. It is our experience that if the individual who champions a BI system is low in the organizational hierarchy he or she may not be able to promote the system. Since a BI system requires the participation and endorsement of everyone in the firm, from the top decision-makers to those lowest in the organization, someone low in the organization will not have the authority and credibility required. A BI system will work only if a person with high credibility manages the implementation. It is desirable that such a person have the endorsement of top management and that this fact be known in the organization.

Training Executives in the Tasks of BI

Training executives to think BI is quite different from training the BI staff in their specific skills. The purpose of executive training is to sensitize the manager to the need for using intelligence in making decisions. Such training should be done as early as possible in the executive's education. Indeed, the ideal would be to introduce future executives to BI during their BA or MBA studies, and then reinforce it through executive development programs. Unfortunately, business schools are only recently becoming aware of this need. One of the pioneering schools in this area is New York University, where a course in BI system design is now part of the MBA curriculum. Other schools should follow in the next few years.

There are standard strategy computer simulation games used in business schools and seminars that can be used to introduce the players to the issues involved in gathering and using intelligence. The authors used one that allowed them to emphasize specific areas of business (in this case, intelligence) over others in the game. The game included an intelligence "market" where companies could purchase intelligence on specific CINs and allocate funds to protect their own information.

Business students who played the game showed a marked increase in awareness of the need to collect and use intelligence and of its role in formulating an overall strategy. Indeed, when the game ended, participants reported that making decisions about what intelligence to buy and how to interpret available information was as important to their game as the making of marketing and financial decisions. This sort of game can be extremely useful in creating the right corporate climate toward BI and in training executives to use intelligence in their decision making.

Final Word: The Role of the Consultant in System Implementation

There are two ways a consultant can help design and implement a BI system.

1. The consultant diagnoses the situation and prepares a report with recommendations, which the company then has to adopt and implement. The consultant may begin with an audit to diagnose existing BI practices, and then follow with comprehensive audit interviews to uncover intelligence needs, identify pockets of information and potential collectors, and describe methods of communicating information. This culminates in a report recommending how the company can improve its BI effectiveness. The report may include recommendations on how to set up the collection network, what information sources to obtain, how to establish a computerized business intelligence data base, what organizational structure the BI system should have, and what the personnel requirements are for the BI operation.

2. The consultant helps the company effect change through its own personnel. The consultant gives help, guidance, advice, and training on a continuing basis, but leaves the organization's own personnel to take the necessary actions. Thus, the consultant may train the company's personnel to conduct an audit and analyze its results, but it is the company's employees who conduct the audit interviews. The consultant may train employees in methods of competitive analysis and data collection. The consultant may also play a significant role in educating executives, users, and collectors in the process of business intelligence (that is, he would conduct intelligence awareness briefings). In addition, the consultant provides criteria for evaluating the progress of BI system implementation and its effectiveness, and from time to time the consultant monitors the company's progress and evaluates the success of the implementation process himself.

The second method is, in our opinion, preferable in implementing a business intelligence system. The implementation of a business intelligence system is a process that takes place over a long period of time. It is not unusual for a BI system—including a collection network, an analysis group, and a computer system—to take several years to be fully implemented and working smoothly. Because of this, it is the role of the consultant as educator, guide, and monitor of progress that is most important to the company. Of course, the first method can be useful, too, especially for a company that has no one who could initially take over the BI responsibility or for a company facing a very complex task in implementing a BI function.

11

Business Intelligence in the Small Firm

Many of the ideas discussed throughout this book have ready applications to the small firm. The organizational environment of a small business, however, calls for adapting the tools and methods of the BI system with some modifications. The nature of the entrepreneur requires unique considerations in designing the BI system for the small firm.

We start by discussing the importance to the entrepreneur of a planned approach to the BI process. The fact is that the spread of the new approach to BI has taken place mainly in the big corporation. A study has shown that over 70 percent of the Fortune 500 firms have instituted some kind of formal BI system. Moreover, other studies show that senior executives at big corporations believe that formal BI is essential to quality performance. At the same time, entrepreneurs and small business owners are much less inclined to see the importance of formal collection and analysis of environmental information. A study by the *Harvard Business Review* revealed that four times as many large businesses train their employees in formal intelligence-gathering techniques than smaller firms.

The lack of formalization of BI activities at small companies does not reflect an aversion to the activity itself. As a matter of fact, entrepreneurs are constantly engaged in surveillance of the environment for opportunities and threats. A recent study by Sumantra Ghoshal (1985), a doctoral student at MIT, revealed an interesting relationship between entrepreneurial traits and intelligence activities. Executives with entrepreneurial orientation were found to consider BI to be relatively more important than executives with a more managerial or "trustee" orientation. The entrepreneurial type concentrated much more on scanning the competitive and market environments than the other group, which distributed its intelligence gathering evenly across several other domains, such as regulatory, resources, and social. The managerial group relied more on opportunistic surveillance of the environment than on an active search triggered by problems or long-range goals. The picture that emerges from the study is that entrepreneurial executives are very actively engaged in BI but are focused on scanning the immediate environment. The ability of the small firm to respond quickly to changes in the market is critically dependent on such surveillance. Yet a price is paid in neglecting the broader arena where social, political, economic, and regulatory trends produce changes that in the long run may prove fatal to the small firm.

If entrepreneurs are very active in gathering and using intelligence, why is there such a marked aversion to formalizing the activity in their firms? There seem to be two main reasons for that attitude among entrepreneurs: First, many are concerned about the ethical and legal issues involved in the collection of intelligence, and second, there is a widespread belief that a formal BI activity is too costly, and only large firms can afford to engage in it.

In a recent forum of company presidents (Gibson 1986), an executive of a material-handling firm complained about the unethical methods used by his competitors to gather intelligence. He cited a case where a research firm, hired by one of his competitors, interviewed him under false pretenses. Fortunately for him, the incident only served to emphasize how important it was to track the competition. To many other small business owners, however, the reluctance to formalize business intelligence is based on their misperception of intelligence collection as a form of industrial espionage.

In many cases, the reluctance to institute a formal BI process is combined with the attitude that what is really important is that the company provide a good product at a low or competitive price. What the competition is doing is therefore, at best, of secondary significance. While no one will deny the importance of finding a niche in the marketplace, it is the deployment of an effective intelligence network that ensures that the company retains its niche. A classic example is the previously mentioned case of EMI, the British company that introduced the medical scanner, and lost its lead very quickly to a host of competitors. The product was good, but the company's surveillance and assessment of the developments in its own market were woefully inadequate.

Another major concern is that of the cost of a BI system. Entrepreneurs believe that a full-scale BI function requires resources beyond their reach, including staff that they cannot spare and a large and sophisticated computer operation. Although it is true that some corporations spend $500,000 or more to track their competitors, those firms may be facing a large number of competitors in dozens of product lines. Moreover, computerizing the BI process is but one of several steps in systematizing the activity. For a small company with relatively limited data requirements, computerizing the system is not necessarily the most urgent step. Moreover, with the growth of software for small PCs, there is much less reluctance to using "high tech" in BI. More and more, small companies are learning to use the computer in their operations.

The Adaptation of the Business Intelligence System to the Smaller Firm

In the chapter on critical intelligence needs, we presented a framework for the use of intelligence in decision making. The concept of CINs applies to both large and small companies. Intelligence gathered by the small firm serves to support decisions regarding pricing strategy and trade discounts, sales targeting, new product introductions, new packaging, promotions, and changes in selling techniques. Entrepreneurs quoted in the presidential forum mentioned above (Gibson 1986) noted the use of intelligence in cases such as quality improvement and cost reduction in their product brought about by reverse engineering of their competitors' products, the smoothing of production cycles, better product positioning, the avoidance of mistakes made by competitors, as well as the duplication of their more successful programs.

The procedure of establishing CINs is even easier in smaller firms than in the large corporation. The use of an audit for that purpose is simple and consensus about the important targets to monitor emerges rapidly. We recommend, however, that the scope of the scanning be explicitly expanded to include the monitoring of broader issues beyond the immediate business domain. Contrary to the belief that such scanning is a luxury in which only corporate staffers can engage, it is the long-term survival and growth of the small firm that may be compromised by neglecting the broad socio-political-demographic-technological picture.

Instituting BI in the smaller firm entails, above all, issuing procedures that direct the inflow and outflow of intelligence. But the procedures must be flexible. There is a lot to be said on behalf of informal BI in the smaller firm. The informal activity is often quicker in transmitting data, the motivation and initiative of employees are high, and *rigid* formalization is unnecessary. Some formalization is important, though. Formalization prevents the phenomenon of "Leave it to George to do," which ends with no one doing the job. Simple procedures can also ensure that data reaching one employee but that are useful to another are disseminated. According to one study (Ghoshal 1985), up to 60 percent of environmental information received by employees is also relevant to other employees. Thus, procedures that require intelligence reporting from the field, by field personnel such as salespeople, are basic to the small firm.

In addition to procedures, the formalization of BI does not entail high expense and a full-time unit. The responsibility for BI can be an addition to an executive's job, with the help of a part-time clerk who will do such things as coordinating and filing of competitive information. In several successful entrepreneurial ventures with which we have worked, this responsibility was undertaken by the company's president. The act clearly represented the importance the entrepreneur attached to receiving intelligence from the different parts of the organization. Since decisions in the smaller firm are typically more centralized than in the large firm, the CEO's need for intelligence is the greatest. Not surprisingly then, the CEO may want to coordinate the BI activities of the various departments and individuals to ensure an adequate supply of intelligence.

The issue of the cost of acquiring intelligence is highly exaggerated. The goal of the internal collection network is to tap the best sources of intelligence—the customers, suppliers, bankers, distributors, and competitors themselves—through the use of the people who are constantly in touch with these sources. The best research company cannot duplicate the day-to-day contact with the market of the company's own personnel. Therefore, setting down a few rules, and perhaps training the employees to recognize and interpret intelligence, is all that is needed by the small firm in this area.

Moreover, the cost of good published sources that cover the market, competition, technology, and broader issues is reasonably low. *The Wall Street Transcript,* for example, offers speeches by corporate executives, and reports by brokerage firms on listed firms, for a few hundred dollars per year. Computerized information services, such as the Dow Jones News Retrieval Service, which offer the entrepreneur the opportunity for a customized search for intelligence on competitors, are inexpensive. Subscription to trade publications is part of the cost of doing business, anyway, and the real issue is whether or not they will be monitored closely enough for opportunistic information. The internal network solves that problem.

In short, cost and sophistication are not the essential features of an effective BI system. For the smaller firm, procedures and training that will increase awareness to BI needs may be sufficient to augment the informal networks and overcome some of the pitfalls of relying solely on them.

Finally, a point regarding the use of reverse competitive analysis technique (RCAT) by the smaller firm. RCAT is a competitive analysis of the firm, performed by the firm itself. Because it involves self-examination, it is termed "reverse" competitive analysis. The researcher performing the RCAT conducts the analysis of the firm using published and field sources, but the investigation is carried out without the prior knowledge of the firm's own personnel. The analysis reveals the way the firm is perceived from the outside, and the intelligence that a competitor could obtain on its strategy, strengths, weaknesses, and future plans. We believe that the RCAT is of great use to the entrepreneur. The reason has to do with the economics of being small and new in the market. The success of a small or a new venture lies directly with its ability to defend its market niche. Unlike its larger competitors, the performance and viability of the small firm do not depend on capturing a large market share, but on keeping the larger competitor from encroaching on its small but profitable one. The economics of entry and survival of the small firm dictate that its larger competitors perceive a fight for the niche as unprofitable. The assessment of its own competitive positioning vis-à-vis the entrepreneurial firm will determine, to a large extent, the larger corporation's willingness to fight and its strategy in fighting the smaller company or the newcomer. It follows that creating the right perception about the small firm's potential, intentions, strategy, and capabilities is crucial for the entrepreneur. The RCAT enables the small firm to determine how it is perceived by the outside world, especially competitors, but also industry experts, government officials, and suppliers. Finding out in which areas the company is considered strong and in which it is considered weak should direct the entrepreneur in setting the grand strategy. Sometimes a company may find out that the competition is not "buying" its message, while other times a company's efforts in a particular area are judged as determined and effective, and the competition gives up on the idea of winning this market away from the firm. Just as the perception of the firm by its clients is considered of paramount importance, the perception (or misperception) by competitors is a great practical piece of information. It may mean the difference between a competitive strategy that creates and defends a niche, and a crowded market where the margins are no longer sufficient to survive.

12

Legal, Moral, and Counterintelligence Issues

The question of what is, and what is not, legal and ethical in business intelligence activities is also the question of how to distinguish industrial espionage from business intelligence. The subject of industrial espionage leads by implication to the issue of internal security, or counterintelligence. Therefore, both topics are included in this chapter.

Ethical Considerations in Business Intelligence

A *Harvard Business Review* survey by Jerry Wall (1974) asked 1211 executives a number of questions regarding business intelligence activities. One of the questions posed to the respondents was aimed at measuring their approval of various intelligence-gathering activities. The activities that were measured ranged from subscribing to a trade journal (98 percent of all respondents approved of this) to wiretapping competitor's phones (only 1 percent approved). The ethical status of the activities between those two extremes was perceived as much grayer. The respondents were split accordingly. Thus,

205

the activities of asking salespeople to report intelligence, the collecting of intelligence at a trade show, and that of buying competitors' products received very high rates of approval. Activities such as hiring away a key employee from a competitor, posing as a prospective customer, or wining and dining a competitor's manager for the purpose of extracting intelligence received split votes. Activities that were clearly unethical and illegal, such as paying a competitor's employee for information, stealing plans, or secretly recording conversations in the competitor's office, were approved by a very low percentage of the managers surveyed.

These results are by now dated and one wonders if and how morals have changed in the last decade with growing competitive pressures. Yet, our experience with managers whose areas of responsibility included BI activities suggests that overall, the American manager is an honest and ethical person. A director of international operations once told us how shocked he was to discover the ease with which he could obtain confidential competitive intelligence in several countries in South America, and even in European countries such as Italy, if only he were willing to pay for it. In fact, he commented that he was *expected* to buy such intelligence as an accepted way of doing business there.

During our public seminars, we have had the occasion to discuss unethical espionage activities with groups of senior managers and corporate intelligence analysts. In those discussions, they repeatedly expressed the belief that "I will not do it, but I am sure some other managers might." The perception of the "other manager" as less ethical is found in Wall's survey as well. It makes you wonder, if all these executives were as ethical as they claimed—we had no reason to suspect their integrity—what was the reason for the common perception of the "unethical executive"? One factor behind this prevailing perception may be the widespread practice of using business intelligence firms, consultants, market research companies, and other experts to prepare market and competitor studies. Some of the methods used by some of these specialists, whose business survival depends upon getting as much intelligence as possible, may not be wholly ethical. For their part, many executives prefer not to know how the information has been obtained, thereby maintaining their own sense of integrity and morality.

In questioning those executives about their own criteria for what was ethical in BI and what was not, several suggested the following popular rule of thumb: "If you do not want to see it as a headline in the newspaper the next morning, do not do it." The answer is sound advice, because newspapers reflect current mores, and these change over time. Though BI activities were considered exotic or unacceptable a decade ago, the contemporary business and social consensus considers BI activities a necessary and effective management practice.[1]

There is no doubt that certain activities are more ambiguous than others where ethics are concerned. Is it ethical to try and force confidential information from a job candidate? The obvious answer is no. But what if the candidate himself initiates the transfer of information? What about the engineer who contacted his competitor, an executive of a large food company, and asked for a job interview? During the interview he pulled out several drawings of a confidential nature and spread them on the desk in front of the executive.

The executive who told us the story claimed that he declined to review the drawings and instead immediately returned them, and that he naturally refused to hire the engineer. His explanation was enlightening: He was concerned that the man could do the same with secrets of his new employer.

But what if the stakes were so high that the possibility of looking at the information could pay off handsomely, even if you wouldn't normally have hired the engineer? Perhaps the best principle is simply that business and personal morality should not be separated. "This is business!" is a common phrase used to justify unethical acts. If an executive will not tolerate the kind of behavior described above among his friends, and won't think of following such low standards in his personal life, he shouldn't succumb to temptation in his business conduct, nor tolerate it among his employees, profit considerations notwithstanding.

Interestingly enough, in a recent survey (Timmons et al. 1985, pp. 158, 184) of 60 successful entrepreneurs whose companies ranged from four million to one billion dollars in sales, the majority claimed that the attribute of integrity was the single most important factor in their long-term success. Over 72 percent said that ethics could and should be part of a business education curriculum. Assuming that for entrepreneurs, even more than for corporate executives, business decisions involve high stakes and sometimes financial survival, their

[1]BI activities are today routinely portrayed in a positive light in the business press. See, for example, *The New York Times*, October 28, 1985: "Keeping tabs on competitors."

emphasis on ethical business behavior is surprising and heartening at the same time.

Industrial Espionage

The reader might have noticed that we've said nothing so far about the legal side of BI activities. That is because we consider the ethical issues to be stricter: Not everything that is legal is ethical. For example, wining and dining a competitor's secretary in the hope of getting intelligence is considered by most executives to be unethical. At the same time, it will be an exceedingly hard task to prosecute the case in court.

The legal issues involved in BI defy easy generalization. There is no federal law regarding BI activities, and the state laws that govern the subject vary greatly. Parker's (1984, pp. 294–304) advice to executives is to plan their BI operation keeping in mind that in case of a challenge, the operation will be reviewed with perfect hindsight. He naturally warns executives to consult their corporate counsel as early as possible to ensure that BI operations are structured so as to prevent future legal problems.

This advice may be sound, but our experience suggests that in reality, things do not work perfectly. Many executives in charge of BI operations testify to the lack of cooperation from their legal departments. Far too many counsels take the easy route, advising unreasonable restrictions to BI activities. That might be good conservative legal advice, but it does not fit the times, nor the real needs of corporations. As a result, executives simply bypass or ignore the legal department altogether. If you don't have a counsel who is current on management tools and practices, you might be better off relying on your common sense, written guidelines, and the fact that legal challenges to BI activities are mostly confined to clear acts of espionage, not to legitimate collection activities.

Your common sense should tell you that obtaining trade secrets is illegal, that finding out the prices of competitors may involve you in an antitrust suit, and that hiring a key employee from a competitor may lead to a legal fight over your ability to use the knowledge of the new employee. In most of these cases, the nature of the information, how well protected it was, and how it was acquired were at the center of the legal investigation.[2] Do not let these considerations paralyze you. True, sending a plane to take photographs of a plant under construction was ruled illegal by the court,[3] and buying stolen trade secrets from employees is clearly illegal,[4] but these are not what the internal intelligence network is all about. An effective BI system does not need to steal or spy. Intelligence data are gleaned by employees during their legitimate job activities, through contacts with customers, suppliers, competitors' employees, and others. Resorting to industrial espionage is the act of a thief, not of a BI specialist.

A written statement about the legality and ethics of BI activities in the corporate policy guide is desirable. One Fortune 500 company that published a section on BI in its code of ethics includes in this section a paragraph about the importance of BI activities, and then reminds employees of the need to maintain accepted standards of legality and fairness in collecting intelligence from nonpublic sources.

Educating employees about trade secrets is another useful measure. A trade secret is any information that gives a company an advantage over the competition who doesn't possess it. According to Steven Mitchel Sack (1985, p. 39), an attorney-at-law, if a company has spent a significant amount of money in creating this information (be it a formula, a device, or something of this nature), is taking precautions to guard the information, and has informed employees about the nature of the information, and the information is not publicly known, then the information may be declared a trade secret by the court.

Finally, it should be kept in mind that legitimate BI activities do not end up in court, and for a good reason. Collecting information on competitors is an accepted part of the business game, and is viewed as a strategic tool by almost all executives and companies. It is when the unspoken laws of the game are broken that legal steps might be taken, not when information is collected per se. Stealing, bribing, using electronic surveillance, or snatching employees solely on the basis of their knowledge of trade secrets are acts that clearly violate the accepted modus operandi of the BI game. Piecing together public and field data collected through monitoring and researching will hardly ever be challenged in court.

[2]For more detail, see Parker (1984, p. 298).
[3]Du Pont v. Christopher, 431 F.2d 1012 (5th Cir.) (1970).
[4]Examples are the attempt of Hitachi and Mitsubishi to buy secret data stolen from IBM in 1982.

Counterintelligence

Even though most American managers are honest and ethical in their approach to competitive intelligence gathering, some are not. Moreover, foreign companies and governments are less concerned about using industrial espionage. Taking measures to protect the company from illegal spying operations is as elementary as installing a burglar alarm in one's own house. Counterintelligence procedures are also effective against legitimate intelligence activities of rivals, though one must always balance those measures with the need to be exposed to the financial community, customers, and regulators.

A typical counterintelligence program can be divided into two components: (1) technical measures, and (2) the human factor.

Technical Measures

A counterintelligence program involves several physical safeguards to guard data. These include:

Installing disposal devices for confidential information. Such devices include shredders, disintegrators, incinerators, or pulping equipment. Some of these devices are large, noisy, and expensive and are suitable for companies with severe security problems. Shredders, on the other hand, should be elementary office equipment. In addition, microfiche melting devices and computer disk disposal methods should be considered for companies storing sensitive data on these media.

Periodic checks by security experts for wiretapping and bugging. The statistics on the number of commercial bugs planted each year is unpleasant (10,000 per year is reported by the *Intelligence Update*, a trade publication of the security industry). A simple preventive measure is to put seals on office telephone junction boxes and other vulnerable points.[5]

[5]A recent article in the British *Journal of Accountancy* (1986, pp. 67–69) presents a more detailed overview of the technological gadgetry one can employ to protect communication lines.

Protecting computer secrecy. Breaches of computer security are rapidly becoming the number one threat to security. An article in the *Journal of Accountancy* (Perschke, Karabin, and Brock, 1986, pp. 104–111) suggests the following measures: Classify data into categories according to their sensitivity, limit access to computer terminals (including using access control software, codes, and passwords), secure the sites housing sensitive data and processing equipment, and use encryption devices for transmission of very sensitive data. Two of the authors, Gerhard Perschke and Stephen Karabin, are employees of the Continental Illinois Bank of Chicago, and their account includes a description of some of the procedures used by the bank. The responsibility for maintaining security, for example, is placed with the systems division, with support from operating units of the bank. A full-scale program is in effect, with its own staff and backing from top management.

Some other technical measures. These include classifying information according to confidentiality, and restricting the distribution accordingly; restricting physical movements of outsiders within the company's facilities; checking the legitimacy of visitors; and conducting periodic inspections of premises for security lapses, such as sensitive data left unlocked overnight.

Instituting background checks on prospective employees. Screening job applicants is always a sound idea. It may prevent problems of dishonest employees, blackmailed employees, and even potential infiltrators. Of course, professionals who attempt to get a job for espionage purposes will have their backgrounds well disguised. But the amateur may be caught.

In dealing with the government, reporting requirements are a serious security risk. The best policy is to divulge only the minimum necessary, and to rely on the limits on freedom of information disclosure to protect sensitive data. One technique is to come to an agreement with the regulating agency in which it will notify the company of an FOI request and allow it to take the necessary steps to prevent a disclosure. Unfortunately, according to Bequai (1985, pp. 17–19), it is axiomatic that government agencies have their "leaks."

The Human Factor

If technical and physical measures are especially designed to fight illegal espionage, attention to the human factor is the key to reducing the leak of legally and ethically collected intelligence. A simple "reverse analysis" of the methods and tools discussed in this book should suggest the best ways to reduce the outflow of intelligence data to competitors. The more significant recommendations are the following:

Educate employees about the subject. Raising the awareness of employees to the intelligence game goes both ways. On the one hand, you are interested that they bring in as much intelligence as possible. On the other, the less they give away, the better. If you go to a trade show or a technical conference intent on collecting information from a competitor's manager, scientist, or salesperson, you should realize that the competitor's employee might be doing the same. Some are better listeners than others: The ability to interview is not distributed equally among people. There are always those people who seem to invoke careless talk in their conversation partner. In this game the winner is the one who can obtain information without giving away too much of his own. Educating employees not to be careless with business information is a long step toward counterintelligence. IBM, for example, has acquired a reputation in this area.

Educating employees involves a myriad of little reminders, memos, posters, articles in the internal newsletter, written policy statements, and an ongoing effort to maintain awareness. The program should address such trivial issues as warnings regarding working on sensitive plans while on the plane or train, leaving confidential files in the car, and shredding typewriter and printer ribbons. Less trivial issues include the content of executives' speeches, promotional literature, patent filing, and court testimony. In all such activities, counterintelligence should at least be a concern.[6]

Create an image and a reputation for toughness. Letting employees and outsiders know that the company is serious about fighting espionage and minimizing intelligence leaks can be a very effective deterrent. Sack (1985) suggests a consistent policy of deterrence including routine confidentiality clauses in employment contracts, effective procedures to insure that departing employees do not take company property with them, and aggressive prosecution of espionage, insider leaks, and ex-employees who use trade secrets in their

---

[6]For additional tips, consult Roy Carter (1986, pp. 7–9), and Richard Eells and Peter Nehemikis (1984).

new careers. An article in *The Economist* (1984) cites several examples of successful prosecution of the latter type: Microcomputer Systems, which sued former employees who founded their own firm and was awarded $2 million, and Fairchild Camera, which obtained a restraining order against a competitor who tried to hire away an engineer with knowledge of Fairchild's secrets. Although the actual success rate in such a prosecution may be low, creating the right image may be as effective as actually winning the cases in court.

Final Word

Industrial espionage is *not* business intelligence. The revolution in organizational thinking about the subject of BI that has been taking place within the last few years reflects the clear understanding of the difference between the short-term gain of the golden eggs and the long-term, strategic resource in the form of the goose. Industrial espionage can sporadically provide some hard-to-get intelligence, but only a legitimate program of business intelligence can systematically scan the environment for opportunities and threats. We encourage you to build up a strategic organizational BI function capable of scanning—not to play a cloak-and-dagger game of spying.

13

Common Problems in Business Intelligence and Their Solutions

We have repeatedly encountered certain problems associated with the design and implementation of a BI system. Through our seminars and our consulting experience we have arrived at various solutions to these problems. This chapter is included in the book as a quick guide to addressing those frequently encountered issues. A more thorough treatment is contained in the relevant chapters.

Sources

1. **No sources.** When a new BI unit is established, one of the first issues that arises is where to obtain information. Even if a BI function has been operating for some time, the range of sources used to glean information may be limited. There are several means by which a varied list of sources can be developed.

(a) An experienced manager can be hired to run the BI system. Alternatively, personnel experienced in BI and the particular industry may be hired to staff the system. They will have an intimate knowl-

214

edge of the industry and will be able to direct the less knowledgeable analysts to the key people and publications in the market.

(b) Through the intelligence audit process and subsequently through the use of the Internal Collection Network (ICN), those directing the BI process can learn about useful sources of information, both published and field.

(c) Even if a formal collection network has not yet been established, it is possible to identify the more prominent experts within the organization and with their assistance compile an initial list of sources.

Beyond this starting point, other avenues can be explored for sources: directories of business intelligence sources, such as those published by Washington Researchers, Find/SVP, or Leonard Fuld; seminars on business intelligence, some of which are oriented to the discussion of specific sources of information; professional and trade conferences and meetings, which can put the BI person in touch with experts in the area of BI or the specific industry. These sources can be a good place to begin when building a network of contacts who will provide leads to additional valuable sources.

2. Too many sources. A BI specialist may sometimes find that the company subscribes to too many sources of information or that too many people send data to the BI office. To compound this, decision-makers may be receiving the data directly and will complain about being inundated with too much data from too many sources. Typically when there is a perception that there are too many sources of information, the problem is not the existence of too many sources per se, but rather that the material provided is irrelevant to the work of the BI group or that the level of detail is too elementary for the needs and objectives of the BI group. As a result, users have to wade through large quantities of irrelevant data; or the data need quite a bit of additional processing to be useful.

The solution to the problem is to carefully evaluate each source or category of sources. As discussed in Chapter 7, evaluating sources for usefulness enables the specialist to eliminate redundant, irrelevant, or overly costly sources. Evaluation may also lead to the conclusion that a source can be useful at another level within the organization, or for a different set of users or BI providers. This conclusion is especially true if the BI system is a complex one with several levels of BI collection, evaluation, and analysis.

3. Unknown quality of sources. If the source is new, its reliability is difficult to determine. There are no miracle solutions to the question of quality of a new source. Commonsense judgments based on the motives and character of a source are the typical approach. Otherwise the source has to be monitored and its performance over time assessed.

4. No field sources. As mentioned throughout the text, the coverage of BI is incomplete if field sources are not tapped. The organization may experience one of several problems in this regard: (1) Field sources are not tapped at all. (2) Information from field sources is used only in a very localized area, its utilization confined to those who gather it. Even though there may be a centralized BI unit, field information does not reach the unit and therefore is not incorporated into whatever intelligence is created by the unit. (3) Contact with field sources is left to BI staff and they find it difficult to get sources to cooperate.

Following are the solutions to each of the problems cited above: (1) The solution to this problem is the creation of a collection network as described in Chapter 5. (2) Since the problem is not one of collection but rather the communication of field information, formal channels should be set up to convey information from field sources. Incentives should be given for passing along field information. (3) If there is no possibility of creating a full-fledged collection network and the task of getting information from field sources is left to the BI staff, there are several things that the BI staff can do to gain access to field sources directly. First, relevant field sources should be identified, then thought given to what will encourage them to talk to the BI staff professional. Why should a supplier or industry expert talk to a BI specialist? Many people will not cooperate, but the few that will could provide valuable information. The analyst may have to give some information in return, especially in talking to consultants and experts who use information as a resource. In general, though, it is the ICN that taps field sources, not the BI specialist. The sources who cooperate with the employees do so as part of doing everyday business. Thus, it is easier for an employee to collect data than for a specialist.

Collection

1. Pockets of information. In most corporations—both large and small—information exists in isolated pockets. A pocket may be a person who does not share information with others (a "gatekeeper"), a department that uses information to its own ends but never passes it along, or a small informal network of employees who exchange information among themselves. This information, although serving the needs of isolated pockets, does not become a true company resource.

The first step in incorporating the informal pockets of information into the formal BI system is the identification of the pockets, done through the intelligence audit (see Chapter 8). The audit maps the existing pockets and details the information they contain. The next step is to conduct an educational campaign to persuade information holders to contribute their knowledge to the common pool: that is, to make the information available to everyone through the formal BI system. In addition to education, proper incentives must be offered, since information is power. If one is to give it up, one must be compensated. The most profitable way to compensate is by placing key people from the "pockets" on the various intelligence committees, so they will have a say in the way the BI system is run and have direct access to information that is provided by others (see Chapter 10).

2. No collection. If a collection network is established, yet information fails to flow through the channels, there are several possible reasons.

(a) There is no incentive to collect. To the majority of employees, collecting and reporting intelligence is an added burden. Unless collection becomes an integral part of the job, through incentives, it will not be carried out as desired. Preaching alone will not do it. Involvement in collection should be rewarded as an element in the total performance appraisal of the employee.

(b) There are problems with communication. Communication methods may be either inflexible, inappropriate, or nonexistent. It is not easy to get employees to report information, even if they already possess ample information that they know could be useful. The solution is to use existing communication channels as much as possible. For example, intelligence reporting can be tagged on to other periodic reporting, and intelligence can be exchanged during department meetings. Another solution is to design a reporting system appropriate for the organization and include reporting as part of the job description.

(c) Conflicts exist with informal networks. Collection and reporting are carried out by managers on a daily basis with their trusted subordinates, peers, and superiors. The informal, loose network is an important part of the politics and power game in the company, and many managers prefer to do intelligence informally and rely on their own networks rather than participate in a company-wide intelligence effort. There is no easy way to overcome resistance to sharing information beyond the personal network. The common advice of organizational change experts is to educate, encourage, and enforce. The three Es can be effective only with solid support from the top level. An additional solution that does not depend on continuous pressure from above is to involve as many preexisting committees as is practical and to get the key managers to participate in them. If these managers perceive the benefit that can be derived from shaping the BI function, they will enlist their own networks to work for the company-wide BI system.

Dissemination

1. Dissemination of raw data. If users receive a flood of information in the form of newspaper clippings, field reports, articles, magazines, statistics, and so forth, the system is providing them with raw data rather than useful intelligence. The purpose of the BI system is to supply users with intelligence, and to that end the intelligence analyst's role is to serve as an intermediary between collectors and decision-makers by converting the flood of raw data into meaningful intelligence. Dissemination of raw data should be limited to what users perceive as necessary background information and to what they will have time to read. Other pieces of raw data that should be included are those that require immediate action. Users should receive only those intelligence reports that contain information important to them as decision-makers: information that enables them to make decisions more effectively and upgrades their ability to manage. This information should be in a format that will free them to use it directly without assembling and analyzing data.

2. Ineffective distribution. Intelligence reports that do not reach all the interested parties may be underutilized. Distribution based on the casual decisions of collectors or the BI staff regarding who may be interested in the intelligence is not very effective. The solution is to prepare user interest profiles on the basis of the intelligence audit.

The profiles, which can be stored on a computer or in an ordinary file, will then serve to create a distribution list for intelligence reports.

3. Intelligence reports that do not address user needs. All too often intelligence reports are not read or utilized by the users because the reports are inappropriate for their needs. Reports may contain too little specific information to be useful for proposal preparation or as a working tool. The contrary may also be true. Reports can be too long and detailed; they can lack a strategic overview and provide little incentive for the busy manager to plod through pages and pages of analysis.

A BI system with poor output, or a BI system that boasts an extensive product of no interest to users, is a system that serves as window dressing and is ultimately a waste of resources. It is therefore important that, when setting up a BI system, an analysis be made of user needs and requirements, and a dissemination and reporting system set up and geared to user specifications. This can be accomplished through conducting an intelligence audit initially, and on an ongoing basis by plugging into the user base through the users committee, which ensures that reports are user-driven. Companies have taken varied approaches to intelligence dissemination. There may be several types of periodic reports—varying in length, scope, and emphasis—which are disseminated to the appropriate users, based on user interest profiles. Another approach is to emphasize customized reports: that is, on-demand reports that are created at user request. Such reports can then be available to others as well.

4. System output is not used. This phenomenon occurs frequently. Executives, skeptical of the value of formal BI or through sheer habit, reject the output from the formal intelligence system in favor of making decisions based on intuition and their own networks.

Establishing the credibility of the BI system takes time, and there is no quick medicine for resistance. There are several measures that can be taken to help promote the use of the system output. First, if the BI system is headed by an executive with clout and prestige, the output of the system will automatically gain credibility. A personal campaign by the executive to encourage decision-makers to use intelligence reports also helps. Second, advertising within the organization of the availability of services and products of the business intelligence unit will encourage use. Facilitating access to the BI specialist for requests for information and special studies creates a bridge between users and the BI staff function and serves to overcome resistance. Lastly, the system should be adopted by users as their own. This can be accomplished by getting executives involved through the intelligence, user, and analysis committees (see Chapter 10). In the final analysis, though, the proof is in the result: The ultimate tool for encouraging use of system output is good intelligence output. As the network expands and analysis deepens, reluctant managers will find that they can gain an edge by utilizing the resources of the business intelligence function.

5. Users use the BI system incorrectly. When information provided by the business intelligence system is used mostly for packaging proposals and only rarely for learning or initiating and evaluating alternative courses of action, the problem may lie within the BI system and its output. Or the problem may lie deeper. If information is not used for supporting decisions, an evaluation has to be made as to the source of the problem. If it is a matter of reports that do not address user needs, the situation may be corrected by reassessing the information needs of managers. If, however, the problem lies elsewhere—that is, the form rather than the substance of plans and proposals is what matters in the organization—the problem is beyond the control of the BI staff and should be addressed by those higher in the organization.

Storage

1. Inaccessible paper files. Paper files make browsing difficult. In addition, if they are not cross-referenced, which is usually the case, it is difficult to access information from different points of view or through different key words. It is difficult to retrieve information for a report from, for example, both a subject-area point of view and a competitor point of view. The solution is to create a card catalog with cross-references, if resources limit the application of computer technology. If, on the other hand, there are funds to invest in a computerized text-oriented data base management system, the problem of cross-referencing and addressing a topic through multiple keys is resolved.

2. Information storage not centralized. Good business intelligence requires that data from many sources reflecting various angles of the same target be related to gain as complete a picture as possible. This requires some form of centralized information storage and retrieval. Thus, files containing intelligence information that are kept by individual users will not serve the purpose of relating intelligence information to gain a comprehensive view. Similarly, data bases maintained and used separately by the various functional areas are not easily accessible by BI personnel and readily usable.

The solution is to centralize all existing information and data bases under the management of the BI staff.

3. Information stored in people's heads. When no files with competitive information are maintained and the need arises for particular information, the person calls several contacts within the organization who have knowledge of the general area of inquiry. The information obtained in this fashion tends to be nonspecific, colored by opinion and longstanding biases.

This kind of problem exists when there is virtually no formal business intelligence. Therefore, the solution to the problem involves more than just resolving the question of storage. In effect, an entire business intelligence system has to be designed and implemented. This includes setting up a system for collection of information, educating people to release information and pass it along on a timely basis, and designating someone as manager of the BI function.

4. No cross-referencing. This problem is encountered typically with manual systems (paper files), where maintaining a cross-referencing catalog is a time-consuming process. It may also be encountered with small limited-capacity data bases, such as ones maintained on a PC.

When there is a need for extensive cross-referencing the only feasible solution may be a text-oriented data base management system on a mainframe that provides for the accessing of the information through multiple key words.

5. User's limited knowledge of what is available or of how to access the system. Whether the system stores full intelligence reports or just raw data, the stored information should be readily available. It is a mistake to assume that managers will make use of intelligence stored on the computer or in other central data banks (for example, the library) simply because it is available. Experience shows that users may not have thorough knowledge of what is available on the system. Additionally, even if they are taught how to search a data base directly, managers prefer to ask the BI specialists to do the research for them rather than perform the task themselves.

There are several solutions. User interest profiles should be employed to inform users of the availability of particular data for their use. Access to the system should be easy and involve as few commands as possible. Business intelligence unit staff should be available for consultation. Heavy users of information on the data base, such as those regularly involved in the preparation of proposals and major presentations, should be briefed regularly at information meetings conducted by the BI staff on the available intelligence and how it can be retrieved. Some companies that have encountered difficulties in encouraging users to access the system themselves have resorted to a BI staff that handles all data base research requests. This system is feasible when there is enough staff to adequately handle the incoming requests. Otherwise, users should be taught how to access the data base themselves.

6. **Bottlenecks on the input side.** The capacity of a computerized BI system is very large. Both storage and computing power have come down in price to such an extent that system capacity is no longer an issue. The input phase of a computerized BI system may pose problems, however. Input into the system can be labor intensive, because information has to be keyed in manually. An optical scanner can serve most input needs. However, optical scanners are still limited in their capability to scan every type and print, and handwritten material is entirely beyond their capability. There are several solutions to the question of input bottlenecks, depending on the cause of the problem. If the system is designed so that raw data are entered into the system, one should consider the following: (1) Is the information being entered available elsewhere, such as on commercial on-line data base systems, and can these external data bases serve as substitutes? (2) Is it possible to enter abstracts, rather than raw data? (3) Is there information that should not be on the system in the first place? (4) Can information—especially field information—be entered at the remote location where it is collected?

7. **Multiplicity of data bases.** The company may have many data bases that have been established over the years; each structured differently, accessed through different software programs, and perhaps stored on different computer systems. To compound matters, not everyone may have knowledge about the existence of each data base, since departments establish data bases for their own use. Thus, a technical data base established and used by research and engineering may be useful for BI purposes, but no one involved in business intelligence has knowledge of the data base. The solution is to make a list of data bases as part of the intelligence audit. Once the data bases are known they can be evaluated for the usefulness of their

content to BI, and methods can be established to make use of the information they contain.

8. Premature implementation of computerized system. The implementation of a system may be premature, as is often the case for automation of other areas and functions within an organization. A clear understanding of how the BI system as a whole is to be structured and how it will function should exist before setting up a computerized system. It is also preferable that a data base be established after a formal BI system has been functioning for some time and its elements (such as a collection network, user interest profiles, and an analysis function) have been operating.

Analysis

1. No expertise. BI analysis can be hampered by lack of expertise on several levels. There may be a lack of skills in competitor and industry analysis. The BI staff may have only superficial knowledge of the industry, technology, or business environment in which the company operates; or it may be inexperienced in establishing sources of information and using them to collect intelligence data for analysis. Lack of expertise prevents the analyst from understanding the significance of particular data on the one hand, and from providing adequate interpretation and analysis on the other. The solutions to the problem will vary from organization to organization, depending on resources and needs. BI analysts can be drawn from the ranks of those who are intimately familiar with the company's business and then trained in intelligence analysis techniques. Another solution is to hire someone well-versed in intelligence analysis who will rely on an internal network of experts to provide needed in-depth expertise in the industry. Alternatively, BI analysis can be carried out by an analysis task force or committee. Distributing analysis among experts in the organization can bring to the process depth of knowledge that staff analysts may not possess.

2. Biased analysis. Analysis may suffer because of the particular biases of the person conducting it. If substantial and limiting biases are perceived, analysis should be delegated to an analysis committee, at least for major decisions. The sharing of ideas in a typical role-playing analysis session is both beneficial for the analysis itself and politically sensible if the analysis is to be used for making a controversial decision.

3. Analysis by end-users only. In some companies analysis is carried out entirely by managers. The function of the BI system is reduced to collection, evaluation, and dissemination. The problem with the distribution of the analysis task entirely among users is that a major benefit of formalizing the BI effort is lost without the perspective afforded by centralized analysis. To circumvent this problem, the BI specialist should perform at least some of the initial tasks of the analysis stage, such as collating and summarizing data. Then completing the analysis and drawing conclusions can be left to the manager. The ideal situation involves cooperation between the manager and the analyst in preparing analyses. This interaction serves to clarify the needs of the decision-maker and to augment the limited expertise of the analyst.

4. Analysis not geared to user needs. The most common reason for analysis that is divorced from user needs is that the analysis group is located at the "wrong" (from the user's perspective) organizational level. A corporate analyst may have difficulty directing the analysis to the needs of the line manager; analysts within the marketing function may not address the wide issues and concerns of strategic planners. A remedy to this situation will come from examining the pros and cons of decentralizing the analysis function, or by delegating some of the analysis tasks to the end-users themselves (the so-called distributed analysis).

5. Users unaware of their intelligence needs. It is difficult to gear the analysis to user needs if the end-users are ignorant of what their needs are. This situation should be dealt with early on, because managers who are uncertain about what intelligence they need are unlikely to support and contribute toward an intensive, company-wide intelligence program. The intelligence audit is the first step toward raising user awareness. In the audit interview, the specialist guides the user into crystallizing his or her intelligence needs.

Management

1. No locus of responsibility. As with any other function in an organization, business intelligence requires a clear locus of responsibility (that is, someone to coordinate and manage the process of business intelligence). Without this person, no systematic BI can be achieved. The majority of companies that have set out to improve their business intelligence capabilities have learned this lesson. This recognition has precipitated a trend toward a company-wide function headed by an experienced executive. Even when an independent BI unit is deemed unnecessary, the task of coordinating the BI activities of the corporation and the business units is clearly defined as the responsibility of a designated executive. For the smaller firm, the BI responsibility may be one of several tasks assigned to a particular executive.

2. No budget. A BI system costs more than an informal BI program. In addition, the costs of a formal BI system are not buried in other budgets as they may be in informal and random business intelligence activities. Expenditures on BI activities include salaries for a director and analysts, incentives to the ICN, computer resources, publications and other sources of information, and miscellaneous administrative expenses. In the smaller company the BI budget often includes a part-time clerk, a bonus to the executive in charge, and perhaps incentives to employees. Start-up costs include a fee for a consultant in system design, a fee for a BI audit by a specialist, and investment in computer hardware and software. Not allocating a sufficient budget for business intelligence activity can ultimately cost the company more than a proper budget would have. These costs can be hidden; they are often lost opportunities that result from a poor understanding of the company's environment and the inability to anticipate competitors' moves and actions. The cost may be more direct, however. It can be the cost of purchasing business intelligence research services from outside vendors as a substitute for an internal business intelligence program.

3. No commitment by top management. Support by top management is the single most important factor behind the success or failure of a BI system. If such support cannot be mustered, or if it falters after the system is set up, the company will not be able to establish a successful company-wide BI system. Sometimes the BI system is the brainchild of a single senior executive who nurtures it, but then leaves the company, after which the system falls apart. It is therefore important that commitment to the BI system go beyond the enthusiasm of a lone champion.

One method of involving more executives in the intelligence function is to gain their participation in the various committees. Another is to tailor intelligence reports to top management interests and projects. However, the first step may very well be to get top management to listen to an in-house briefing by an outside expert on implementing business intelligence systems. Although top management may in principle agree that there is a need for better business intelligence, they may not know how much organizational effort this will entail. Therefore, little or no budget is allocated. A briefing will present top management with the critical issues and benefits of the system and how they can be achieved organizationally. Knowledge provides sound commitment on which to build the BI effort.

4. No training. The field of BI is relatively new. It is still difficult to find experienced intelligence analysts and other business intelligence experts. The remedies include sending candidates to outside briefings on business intelligence and organizing in-house seminars for the people assigned to the BI unit, as well as collectors, computer personnel, and end-users. The field of business intelligence and competitive analysis is now booming with courses and seminars on the topic and it is easy to find customized training. Several universities have been offering courses on competitive analysis and New York University is beginning to offer a course on business intelligence systems in its MBA program. We expect this trend to continue, as more and more companies seek to hire BI specialists.

Organization

1. Too centralized. A business intelligence system can be structured at either end of a spectrum: completely decentralized or completely centralized. Each type of BI structure is appropriate for certain kinds of companies. A completely centralized BI system can pose problems for a large, multi-unit company, where the divisions compete in distinct markets, produce and market distinct products and technologies, and face competitors unique to each division. The symptoms of an inappropriately centralized BI system are reflected in analysis that is not geared to the needs of the division and is hardly used by divisional managers, limited cooperation of divisional managers and staff with the corporate BI staff, and reluctance on the part of the business units to pick up the tab for BI projects. The solution is to find ways to delegate appropriate BI responsibilities to the business units, and to provide the units with the autonomy to set their own targets and priorities while providing them with consultation and support in the BI effort.

2. Too decentralized. An inappropriately decentralized BI system is one in which the business intelligence effort is scattered among several functional areas and/or business units, but which could function more smoothly and efficiently and be more beneficial to BI consumers if it were carried out by one dedicated group. Symptoms of such a system are intelligence that is generated in one business unit and is not shared with another that needs it, overlapping targets that are nonetheless addressed by each division separately, corporate executives who are distrustful of the data fed to them by the units, and a corporate strategic point of view that is not reflected by BI information compiled by each division separately. The solution is to examine the possibility of a support approach or a combined business intelligence structure (see Chapter 10).

3. Function too low on organizational chart. The location of a BI function within the organization's hierarchy and the locus of responsibility for the BI activity vary considerably from one firm to another. There are BI units staffed with young people who report to a middle-level manager, and there are systems where the units report to an executive just below the president. There are BI functions where the division president acts as the chief intelligence officer. Not surprisingly, the higher the unit is situated within the organization, the more visibility, prestige, credibility, and influence it can have and the more effective it can be in securing cooperation from the total organization. More importantly, if the function is too low in the organization, it is unlikely to obtain an appropriate budget, provide the needed strategic perspective to its intelligence product, or gain enough support to survive in the long run.

4. Function in wrong place on organizational chart. A BI system in one company failed because although it was reporting to a vice president of marketing in the largest division—who was the BI system champion—it was charged with overseeing the BI operation or the entire corporation. Another problem frequently associated with a BI function housed in a marketing department is the emphasis on marketing intelligence, while the needs of users in the organization are more inclusive—especially on the corporate strategic level—requiring thorough consideration of technological, financial, and regulatory intelligence. There is no single location in an organization that is best for a business intelligence unit, but there are several commonsense considerations that can be made. One can examine the fit between the scope of the BI function and the ability of the assigned organizational area to support and market the function. Often the solution is to link business intelligence with the planning department, or to locate it where there is relevant expertise—for example, to expand the market research department to include business intelligence functions.

5. No cross-departmental communication. A BI system that fails to elicit cooperation of salespeople or the marketing department is not going to be very effective. Though it is possible to maintain a BI program that is largely independent of cross-departmental communication (such as a research unit that concentrates on published sources), such a program is not transforming BI into an organizational resource. Sometimes the solution is as simple as having department heads nominate BI supervisors within their departments who are then responsible for better coordination. Sometimes, however, the reluctance to share information is so great that no BI system will overcome it without direct intervention by top management.

6. No divisional communication. Communication among divisions is important if they are related in their businesses and markets and therefore in their information needs. Lack of information sharing between related divisions may not be limited to BI activities, but can indicate a much deeper lack of cooperation. The solution is beyond the level of the BI people and often has to do with a lack of clear-cut corporate policy.

7. Lack of supportive organizational culture. A sophisticated BI system that takes advantage of field information requires the cooperation of everyone in the organization who could provide information. In addition, for a BI system to be effective the intelligence product has to be used by managers and decision-makers. If the organization lacks a supportive culture for intelligence, the goals of the BI process will be difficult to achieve. Creating a supportive organizational culture requires a long educational effort, starting at the top and going down every level in the organization. Top management must be supportive of the intelligence function if it is to flourish. Top management should not only promote the need for better intelligence, but should use the intelligence provided to support its decisions. Others in the organization should be willing and able to collect and transmit relevant intelligence data to the BI function. The main educational tool for creating the appropriate intelligence-sensitive climate in the organization is the BI awareness briefing (see Chapter 5).

8. Too much formality. A system that is too heavily formalized and regulated lacks flexibility and simplicity. A rigid system cannot scan the broader environment for unpredictable opportunities and will take a long time to adjust to changing needs. Too complex a system can also discourage employees from collecting and transmitting data. The solutions are: avoid creating new communication procedures if it is possible to use existing ones; be flexible in methods of reporting (see Chapter 5); consult end-users regularly on their intelligence needs through active committee work (see Chapter 10); and create a flexible intelligence product that can adapt to changing user needs.

Bibliography

Aguilar, F. J. 1967. *Scanning the Business Environment.* New York: Macmillan.

Bales, Carter, et al. 1980. "Competitive Cost Analysis." McKinsey Staff Paper (January).

Bequai, August. 1985. "Management Can Prevent Industrial Espionage." *SAM Advanced Management Journal* (Winter).

Brandenberg, Mary. 1986. "Are Your Premises Free and Clear of Bugs?" *Journal of Accountancy* (July).

Buaron, Roberto. 1980. "New Game Strategies." McKinsey Staff Paper (March).

Carter, Roy. 1986. "Can Your Company Keep a Secret?" *Canadian Manager* (Summer).

Cooke, Terence E. 1986. *Mergers and Acquisitions.* Oxford, England: Basil Blackwell.

Ebeling, H. W., and T. L. Doorley. 1983. "A Strategic Approach to Acquisitions." *Journal of Business Strategy* (Winter).

The Economist. 1984. "A Spy Catcher on the Payroll?" (June 16.)

Eells, Richard, and Peter Nehemikis. 1984. *Corporate Intelligence and Espionage.* New York: Macmillan.

Fry, Joseph N., and Peter J. Killing. 1986. *Strategic Analysis and Action.* Englewood Cliffs, N.J.: Prentice-Hall.

Fuld, Leonard. 1985. *Competitor Intelligence.* New York: John Wiley.

Ghoshal, Sumantra. 1985. "Environmental Scanning: An Individual and Organizational Level Analysis." Ph.D. dissertation, M.I.T.

Gibson, Ray. 1986. "Competitive Espionage." *Small Business Reporter* (May), pp. 32–33.

Gilad, B., and L. Roller. 1987. "Strategic Business Intelligence: An

Experimental Approach." Working Papers Series #16, Rutgers University, Dept. of Business Administration.

Greene, Richard M. 1966. *Business Intelligence and Espionage.* Homewood, Ill.: Dow-Jones Irwin.

Hayes, Robert H., and William J. Abernathy. 1980. "Managing Our Way to Economic Decline." *Harvard Business Review* (July–August).

Miller, Danny, and Peter H. Friesen. 1977. "Strategy Making in Context: Ten Empirical Archetypes." *The Journal of Management Studies* (October).

Montgomery, David B., and Charles B. Weinberg. 1979. "Toward Strategic Intelligence Systems." *Journal of Marketing* (Fall), Vol. 43, pp. 41–52.

Naylor, Thomas. 1980. *Strategic Planning Management.* Oxford, Ohio: Planning Executive Institute.

Naylor, Thomas, John M. Vernon, and Kenneth L. Wertz. 1983. *Managerial Economics.* Englewood Cliffs, N.J.: Prentice-Hall.

Parker, David. 1984. "Legal Implications of Competitor Intelligence," in *Business Competitor Intelligence.* Edited by W. L. Sammon, M. A. Kurland, and R. Spitalnic. New York: John Wiley.

Perschke, G. A., S. J. Karabin, and T. L. Brock. 1986. "Four Steps to Security." *Journal of Accountancy* (April).

Porter, Michael. 1985. *Competitive Advantage.* New York: The Free Press.

———. 1980. *Competitive Strategy.* New York: The Free Press.

Rothschild, William E. 1984. *How to Gain and Maintain the Competitive Advantage in Business.* New York: McGraw-Hill.

Sack, Steven Mitchel. 1985. "You *Can* Keep a Secret." *Sales and Marketing Management* (February 4).

Thompson, Arthur A. 1985. *Economics of the Firm,* 4th ed. Englewood Cliffs, N.J.: Prentice-Hall.

Timmons, J. A., et al. 1985. *New Venture Creation,* 2nd ed. Homewood, Ill.: Dow-Jones Irwin.

Wall, Jerry L. 1974. "What the Competitor is Doing: Your Need to Know." *Harvard Business Review* (November–December), Vol. 52, #6, pp. 1–12.

Index

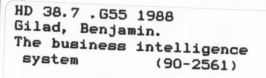